POWER OF POSITIVE THINKING

DR. YADUVIR SINGH

ISBN 979-888521026-3

The book, "Power of Positive Thinking" is dedicated to the God, and to the entire humanity.

Contents

Contents

Contents

Foreword

The book, "Power of Positive Thinking" gives a clear and a very effective explanation of thinking, mind and the karma. The book, "Power of Positive Thinking" is first book of its kind, which discusses all practical aspects related to positive thinking and the life like, psyche, attitude, goals and desires, meditation, behaviour, nature, prayer, the God, right imagination, right job, excellence, real beauty, death and beyond, Moksha etc.. Thinking and Karma always had been very interesting topics full of many secrets, and quite less understood by the majority of beings. Thinking and Karma is the essence of spirituality. Karma is the basis of whole creation. Thinking creates action(s). Thinking and action create Karma. The reader will get to know some amazing facts related to the positive thinking, and its powers, after reading this book, "Power of Positive Thinking". The author has nicely sequenced and described the topics chapter wise. Body, mind and the spirit have been very clearly explained. Effects of right and positive thinking on the life have also been described in a very clear and effective manner. People in general are ignorant of the power of positive thinking. Power of positive thinking is one of the biggest secrets of the life. It opens the secret doors of the universe for a being for getting anything in the life, what he or she wishes for. All highly successful beings use the power of positive thinking quite effectively in their lives. Meditation is the best way to activate and train the subconscious mind. Meditation acts as a data and information filter, and thus, makes a being, more mindful and happier than before. Meditation changes the subconscious mind through improved awareness.

Meditation creates positive thinking. Meditation calms the mind, as the movement of negative thoughts is slowed down, and ultimately stopped. Negativity gets eliminated due to meditation. Meditation and Sudarshan Kriya help clean one's bad karma. Karma is the basis of everything in the life, and also, of the whole creation. Karma creates impressions in the energy, i.e. the energy landscape, which spreads all over in this entire creation. This energy is one's individual consciousness, the universal consciousness and the God. One's thoughts, eventually become his or her spoken words, and then, the spoken words become his or her actions, and finally, actions become his or her personality. It is a gem book on this very interesting topic of power of positive thinking.

This book, "Power of Positive Thinking" makes very lucid discussions about various scientific and spiritual aspects related to the mind and the thinking. People working in the areas of psychology, cognition, neuroscience, religion and spiritualism will find this book as a ready reckoner and a guide, and an important handbook. Definitely this book is a very rich addition in the intellectual closet of the reader. In near future, some more good books on other life important and humanity related topics are expected from the author. The author, every other time, raises his own bar and the threshold, by creating another masterpiece, much to his name and credit. Spiritual beings do not run after success and glory, as it comes to them automatically due to their thoughts and actions. They are under constant divine guidance and blessings, and are being decreed by the God, to do the needed things in their given life.

Definitely, the readers will find it a very interesting book on this rare topic of power of positive thinking, with many takeaways for their implementation in their daily lives.

- Baba
22 / 03 / 2021

Preface

This book, "Power of Positive Thinking" is a comprehensive discussion about the mind, positive thinking, psyche, attitude, goals and desires, meditation, behaviour, nature, prayer, the God, right imagination, right job, excellence, real beauty, death and beyond, Moksha etc.. All successful people use the power of positive thinking, and make all right decisions in their lives. Right decisions are always taken with a balanced open mind based on positive thinking. No decision in the life is either fully right or fully wrong. Seemingly similar thoughts and actions have different results for different beings due to their different worlds. World of a being is the set of his or her life experiences. No two beings have similar experiences and learning, or similar life. Beings come into the existence to live by themselves, and to support others to live meaningfully. Life creates life experiences. Life is an experience in itself. No bad experience is really bad. Discern and differentiate between the correct and the incorrect. A bad decision is just learning, which helps in the growth, evolution and advancement of the soul. In this creation, which is replete with duality, for every good thing, innumerable support logics can be mentioned, and similarly, for every bad thing, innumerable support logic can also be given, interestingly which may not be always incorrect. Life is a game, understand it like a game only, and play it well. Every thought is a creation of being. Thought is energy. Source of thought is information. What is ingested, taken inside, and assimilated, affect the quality of thoughts. One's senses bring the outer things, inside the being. What is seen, smelt, heard, tasted and felt, is created as information by the brain. Brain only does, what the mind says to it. Mind is the master, and brain is its slave. Train and manage the mind in such a way, that negative information is not generated. Positive self-talk is always good, as it promotes being's mental, emotional and the physical health.

Spending time on hobbies improves one's mental health, and also, the overall well-being. Beings with hobbies are less likely to suffer from the problems related to the stress, low mood, and depression. Hobbies make one to feel happier and relaxed. Do mediation and yoga. Make these hobbies. Attitude of gratitude positively affects the brain. Attitude of gratitude develops one's resilience ability towards the challenging situations and the adversities of life. Relationships improve. Network grows. One becomes more energetic, confident and enthusiastic. Power of gratitude is enormous. Be grateful to all other beings, who have positively affected the life. Blessings are received by doing showing sincere gratitude. Thanksgiving is a magical act. Practise various methods of spirituality and empower the self. Empowering the self is advancing the soul, which in turn, results in the start of one's journey on the path of reaching the God.

This book, "Power of Positive Thinking" is a great gift from the author to the entire humanity in today's times, when there is fierce professionalism, immense competition, tremendous fear, overwhelming stress, deepest levels of anxiety, weakest and most fragile bonds of relationships, heightened levels of distrust, hatred and lowest levels of mutual respect, high ego, no self-esteem and dignity, no integrity in actions, biases and prejudices, unethical practices and hypocrisy at their peak, and cynicism getting reflected all over in the human thought process.

This book, “Power of Positive Thinking” is a best pick of its times from the bookstore, and a must read for all. I wish all the readers, a happy reading experience while going through every word, line, paragraph and chapter of the book, “Power of Positive Thinking”. Reader will feel empowered while reading this book. Power is always of the soul. It is the power of the mind, which runs the whole show of life. Reader will not be able to stop, reading it again and repeating many chapters. Read and explain the book to the members of family, relatives and friends, and gift this book, “Power of Positive Thinking” to them, and also, to all others to whom you love and care.

- **Dr. Yaduvir Singh**
25 / 02 / 2021

Acknowledgements

The contents of this book, “Power of Positive Thinking” are the results of understanding and experiences of the author on this topic. However, one may always differ from that, what is written. Also, author tenders his sincere apologies in anticipation, if any content is contrary to their faith, belief, knowledge, information, experiences, and hurts their sentiment in any manner. The author will like to acknowledge, all visible and invisible forces, and powers of this existence for providing information, experiences, encouragement and support. The author will like to acknowledge all sources of information, which gradually developed author’s understanding about the power of positive thinking over many years, along with the experiences. The author also disclaims the responsibility for any loss or damage or harm, if any. Last but not the least, and also, much above everything and all, nothing is possible without the God’s will. Author with full servility, respect, gratitude and surrender to the God, puts this book, “Power of Positive Thinking” on the feet of the God. All is of the God only.

Prologue

This book, “Power of Positive Thinking”, is a gem in itself, a marvellous intellectual creation par excellence, and a must read book for all, and also, a worthy collection. It is a rare book on a very interesting topic i.e. the power of positive thinking. This life, nature, universe and the entire creation are too intriguing and mysterious. This book, “Power of Positive Thinking” discusses mind, positive thinking, psyche, attitude, goals and desires, meditation, behaviour, nature, prayer, the God, right imagination, right job, excellence, real beauty, depression, death and beyond, Moksha, and many other important and relevant topics related to the mind, thinking and the karma. A reading of this book, “Power of Positive Thinking” will develop the reader’s proper understanding about the mind, thinking and the karma. The book, "Power of Positive Thinking" has given simple explanations of various aspects related to the mind and thinking. The reader will find the book too involving, informative, and also, recreational. Books are the best friends of human beings. Book makes a reader travel through all its contents, and experience the whole journey of reading by him or herself even without lifting the feet. Loosen up, and lose yourself in the book, “Power of Positive Thinking”, find yourself there, and get benefitted in the life. Keep learning in the life.

CHAPTER ONE

Thinking

Thinking is the basis for everything in this life and the creation. Thought has created this universe. You, me and everything, in essence, are thoughts only. It is the thought, which creates fiction, figments of imagination, and one's perceived realities as the experiences of life. Life is a thought. Thoughts are created by the consciousness. Consciousness is energy. Energy creates thoughts. God is a thought only. Thoughts create one's world. One's family, relatives, neighbours and friends, all are thoughts only. All relationships are thoughts. Thoughts create Karma. The quality of one's thoughts, determines the quality of his or her life. Thinking is a cognitive process. Consciousness creates thinking. Brain simply does, what the mind tells it. Stop overthinking and overanalyses. Too much thinking does not help. Every thought must be succeeded by its action, otherwise, thought is futile. Stop thinking, and start doing. Walk the talk. Positive thinking results in positive karma, i.e. good karma. Positive thinking not only brings physical and spiritual success in one's life, but also, offsets his or her negative karma, which is the ultimate goal of life. Thoughts must be constructive in nature, meant for well-being of the entire creation. Thinking is emergence of ideas, or formation of opinions about something. Think high, and feel deep. Learn to live and survive alone. Everything is ephemeral. Think of the God. Think of the beauty inside, and the outside, and the world will change and become beautiful. What we think, we become. Mind should be made free of thoughts by regularly doing Dhyana (concentration of mind), prayers, meditation, yoga, playing sports, and doing the physical exercises. A thinking mind is the source of all evils. One's deep connections with the nature, and the appreciation of the creation, calm down his or her mind. Use the power of the subconscious mind. It is the kind of thinking only, which brings either the happiness or the unhappiness in one's life. Think big. Be truthful, kind and helpful. Never act without thinking, but if thought something, definitely act on it. Thinking is beginning, and the action is the end. Thoughts and actions are bound to one another. Both, creativity and intelligence are thinking. Every moment of the life, is a thought. Create the kind of moment, as wished for, with proper thinking. Think less, but right. Think clear, with no confusion(s). Have the courage to reject. Bring clarity to thinking. Life becomes too simple and straight, once these confusions of thoughts and thinking are being worked upon and eliminated. Work on desires and fears. A proper thinking brings stability, and an improper thinking impairs, and brings instability. Be plain, and not complex. It will keep the mind calm and peaceful. Life is in the present moment, and it is neither in the past, nor in the future. Be courageous. This life is for those beings, which have winning thoughts and thinking, and the right attitude. Whatever is thought repeatedly, happens.

CHAPTER TWO

The Psyche

Psyche is mind. Psyche is one's deepest feelings and attitudes. Psyche has three components, viz. conscious (fully known and fully aware), subconscious (less known and less aware), and the unconscious (totally unknown and totally unaware). Ponder the situation, which is needed in the life. Envisage it. One can create the kind of life, he or she wishes for, just by repeatedly thinking about it. Present circumstance and situations may not be promising, so exclude them, and think and rethink of a better situation in the life. Think repeatedly, as what is wished for, comes or happens in the life. Subconscious mind is very powerful, and once it receives the information, it starts working on it, in order to create or bring it in the life of being. There are many secrets, and the secret doors, in this universe. Subconscious mind has capability to open these secret doors. Positive thinking greatly affects being's psyche. It is the power of thinking. A being is an embodied mind with enormous cognitive capacity. Radiate positivity always. Practise positive thinking in order to achieve the goals of life, while excluding all possible negativity. Affirm great destiny for self. Thoughts and words affect, and have impact on the psyche. Learn to deal effectively with your imperfections. Increase life energies. Live happily. Psyche is a part of the life, and not the life, yet it largely controls and runs the life.

CHAPTER THREE

Mind And Thought

Do mind management. Life is all about mind management. There is a certain mental diet, which is needed regularly by the mind. Mind and thought are connected with one another. Thoughts are quite powerful. One should know, how to control the mind. Peace of mind is very much essential for a happy life. Work on self. Maintain physical, emotional and mental well-being. Give time to self. Overcome fear and anger. Eliminate all the struggles of thoughts and life, going on in the mind. Keep energies up with good thoughts and actions. Keep vibrations strong and positive. Aura must be clean, pure and strong. Make mind more and more powerful. Situations should not affect the beings, but beings should affect the situations. Do not get influenced by others. Be influential. State of mind of a being, should be under full control, and as per the choice of the being. Mind should not get disturbed by the situations, problems and circumstances of the life. All situations, problems and circumstances of the life are created by the mind. Change the mind, and these situations, problems and circumstances will also change. Work on "I". Be witness to self. Only, being is the examinee, and also, the examiner, of his or her life, and no one else. Remove all the fears and insecurities of the life, which are created by the mind.

Nothing is for real and permanent in this temporary and ephemeral journey of life. Life is infinite, but every journey of life is too short. Everything is unreal. One's world is set of his or her life experiences, which is a fallacy. Every being has his or her different experiences, so his or her world is also different. There are many worlds within a world for each being. This all, is creation and play of mind. Be the director, and direct the mind to act as a hero, and not as a villain for yourself. Thoughts should be clean, clear, pure, intense and strong. Thoughts are created by the mind. Be calm and peaceful, and you will become winner in the game of life. Do Dhyana, Yoga, meditation, prayers, physical exercises etc., for physical and mental agility. Play sports regularly. Drink lots of water. Eat good and limited food. Keep good friends. Read good books. These all, help maintain the sync among the body, mind and the spirit. Yoga has the ability to make a being, more and more conscious from within. There should be no confusion and conflict in the mind. Train your mind this way. Use power of affirmations. Life conditioning should be proper. Keep your desires and fears too limited in the life. Live happily and keep others happy. One's world is his or her living environment. Life has no set or definite purpose. Life must be explored. Life is the gift of the God. Give respect to it, and live the life with great honour, self-respect, self-esteem and the dignity. All this is just a thought. Thought is the very basis of life. Thought is the basis of everything in this creation. Understanding of the creator, i.e. the God is also a thought. This creation was created out of a thought. We are created out of thoughts. Thought is the cause or the input, and rest all, is simply the effect or outcome or output. Thoughts should be deliberate and guided. Thinking should be conscious. Thoughts have the power to eliminate all harrowing experiences of the life. Happy emotions bring happiness, and bad emotions simply laden the beings and make life unhappy. Love, joy, help, charity, benevolence, empathy, sympathy etc. are happy emotions. Hatred, anger, sadness, resentment, jealousy, getting envious, compulsive thinking etc. are bad emotions. Compulsive thinking creates thoughts, which are repeated, persistent and unwanted, and these urges or images are quite intrusive, and cause distress and anxiety in the beings. Emotions are created out of repeated feelings, which keep going inside the mind of the being. One's mind perpetuates his or her thoughts, feelings and emotions. Picture created in the mind, becomes a reality in the life. Thoughts are created in the conscious mind. It is a thought world, which is continuously created inside the mind inside the body, on the basis of the inputs from the body's sense-perceptions. Thoughts, which are repeated, go into the subconscious mind, and become impressions there, as tendencies. These tendencies are also known as the Samskara or Sanskara (संस्कार). Memories are thoughts, which are already there in the subconscious mind, but now brought to, and emerging, in the conscious mind. One's whole set of thoughts (the thoughts world) is either based on his or her memory, or based on the inputs given by his or her sense-perceptions. Thus, the quality and the nature of the thoughts are affected by the quality and nature of one's sense-intake. One's mind input(s), i.e. sense-intake must be noble, pure, unsullied, immaculate and impeccable, in order to have lofty thoughts.

CHAPTER FOUR

Body, Mind And Spirit

Life is a trap. Its escape is only through karma. Body, with mind and spirit inside, is the most sophisticated system on the planet, given to the beings, by the God as a gift. In physical form only, a being can pay off his or her karma, which got created on the physical plane or realm, i.e. earth. Body has been given to experience, and to live, a much fulfilling life. Life must be celebrated at every moment. How the body is being handled, is purely up to the being. One's thinking deeply affects the functioning of the body and the mind. Spirit also gets affected by the thinking, but less, as compared to the effects of thinking on body and mind. It is the power of the positive thinking, which helps, keeping the body and the mind in its best desired states. Lead the life consciously, and by choice, and not just accidentally. It is the power of Yoga and meditation, by which thoughts are being controlled, and thus, the life is being consciously led. Yoga makes a being more and more conscious, and thus, increases the extent of his or her conscious mind. The sync among the body, mind and the spirit must remain established in its best form and format always, in order to explore the life and the creation in its fullness. Live the life in full exuberance. Life should not let go as a waste. Body helps in achieving the goals of the life. Body is matter, mind and the spirit are energies. Body, mind and the spirit, is an association of matter and energy. Before birth and after the death, a being remains in the energy form. The purpose of the birth is to enjoy the physicality in the physical form (bodily form), pay off all the karma, and advance the soul. The purpose of the life is to raise the present level of the consciousness. Memories are, repeatedly emerging subconscious mind thoughts, in the conscious mind. Memories should be good, never negative, but always positive. Erase bad memories and bad experiences of life, from the mind, by mind management. Raised level of consciousness, not only regulates the memories, but also, being's sense-perceptions. Thus, what one sees, smells, hears, tastes, and touches and feels, must be of very high standards. It is very much necessary for a positive mind, leading to positive thinking. Repetitive thoughts are manifested in life, therefore, work on the mind and the thoughts, based on the kind of manifestations, which are wished for, in the life. Dhyan, Yoga, meditation, physical exercises, sports, healthy life style and other good practises, are the methods and the techniques, for maintaining a strong rhythm and balance in the journey of life, while keeping the harmony among body, mind and the spirit.

CHAPTER FIVE

What Is Life

Every being is the spark of the same infinite. We all are children of the God. Become fearless. Remain undaunted. We all are alone, however, the God always accompanies us. Creation is an outcome of variations and disturbances in the universal consciousness. Every being is an individuated energy, which got separated, from the supreme energy i.e. the God, for the purpose of getting physical experiences and life learning. Life is an experience in itself. Physical plane (earth) is training school for spirits. Beings are spirits. Spirits come here on physical plane from the Spirit World, assume bodily form (physical form) by taking birth, go through all ups and downs in the journey of life (lessons and experiences), and then, return back to the Spirit World at the time of death. Spirit World is true and permanent home of all beings. Beings are spirits (energy), and not the body (matter). Life keeps on repeating the lessons, till these assigned lessons for the given journey of life, are not being learnt properly by the being's spirit. Life is a game, play it well. Stay on the pitch of life, and do not leave this pitch in between on your own volition or seeming compulsions. Here, in the game of life, in essence, there is nothing like success or failure, or gain and loss, but all is just a drama in the journey of life, therefore, enact the allotted role well. Just witness the drama of the life. Every journey of life has its own script. This script is also not same, but changes from one lifetime to other lifetime. In this ever expanding and changing universe, nothing is for real. All is dynamic, changing in time and space, temporary and ephemeral. Life and its experiences in the physical plane i.e. earth, is nothing but all about the mind management. Life has its own ethereal music and beauty. Unfortunately, very few enlightened beings are able to, see it, feel and experience it, and live with it. Heaven and hell are, simply the creations of the mind, culminating as the experiences of the life. For such enlightened beings, their sojourn on the physical plane i.e. earth, is truly a fruitful and heavenly experience. For general beings, the understanding of their world, and the all their worldly experiences, are incorrect, and quite painful and miserable, as they fail to realise that all as sensed and perceived by them here on this physical plane i.e. earth, is simply an illusion and unreal. They take all for real, and thus, waste their life. Such souls are poor souls. Life is an illusion. Life has no purpose. Life is a purposeless game, and the show, created by the God. No physical achievement of being is an achievement for the God. Religious and spiritual attainments have their meanings. God wants beings to always thing good and act good, no matter what. There is no caste, creed, religion or any discrimination among the sprits in the Spirit World. Karma is the only basis of differential treatment of spirits in the Spirit World. Mantra of life is, to stay on the pitch of life. Play the life till death, do not stop playing. Keep making efforts. There is nothing like success and failure. Life is performing, and only performing, without caring for the outcomes. Live the life happily, and in love, always. What is here today, will change tomorrow. Why to wish for something permanent, for this temporary life. Eliminate all fears and anxieties of life. These are curses of the life. We are own gods, and our own creators. Do mind management, in order to lead a meaningful life. Understand what the life is. Take the life sincerely, and not seriously. Life is too fragile. Neither it is permanent, nor permanent is any other thing associated with the life. Life is just a certain count of breath. Future is totally unknown. Live in the present moment. If future is known, excitement of life will be soon over. Do not just pass the life, but always celebrate the life. Life is a celebration. Never spoil the present, by recalling the bad past, and fearing about the future. This whole creation is energy. God is energy. Beings are energies. Consciousness is energy. Soul and spirit are energies. Energy never disappears from the universe. Matter and energy can never be destroyed. Both, matter and energy only get transformed, over the time. Life does not create thoughts, rather it is other way round, i.e. thoughts create the life. Life becomes positive, when thoughts are positive. Birth as a human being is not a simple thing, but it was a long journey of that spirit, through many species and other life forms, involving eons and eons of its continuous evolution. This evolution process, even does not stop here, but continues, till the divinity is not attained. Life is a trap. It is a trap of birth-death, and then rebirth. The only escape from this trap of life is good karma, i.e. good thoughts and actions. Nothings stops a being from thinking good and acting good. It is only his or her mind. Make your mind your friend, and not your foe. Let the mind not work against you. Value the life, live the life consciously. Manage and condition the mind, such that it works positively in the right direction of the soul advancement. Life should be a fulfilling and a gratifying experience. Live the life in its exuberance. All successful beings have good mind management, and they practise positive thinking continuously knowingly or unknowingly. Bitterness, jealousy and criticism should have no place in the life. Thoughts are the source of the life. Life is a thought only. This world is a thought. All worldly experiences have emanated from thoughts. The notion of the God is a thought. We wear and carry our thoughts continuously. In life, anything and everything can be done by using the power of thoughts, the positive thinking. Do not lead a compulsive life. Give energy to the positive thoughts. Energy energises and activates that thing, which it is given to. Being's system, i.e. body mind and the spirit, follows his or her thought and the thought process. What we believe, we become. Increase the capacity of the conscious mind, and explore the self, and the life.

CHAPTER SIX

Purpose Of Life

Positive thinking, positive feeling and positive imagination, are the essence of life.One's experiences are what he or she feels repeatedly. That thing, which is felt, is only attracted towards the life of being. It is the Law of Attraction. It works for all, in every case, in every situation, without exception. The purpose of life is to live the life, honour the life, love the life, realise the importance of life, and experience the life. One's purpose of life is knowing one's true self or one's real self. Life is the basis of anything and everything. Knowing the life and its purpose is knowing the God. Life and the God are one and the same. Therefore, finding the purpose of the life is finding the purpose of the God. Mind needs purpose for everything. Mind works against one's wishes. Mind generates fears and insecurities. Knowing the purpose of the life is a creation of one's mind, but remember that the mind deludes. Freedom is requirement of life, and a characteristic of the soul, then why to bind the life and the soul by defining a purpose of to life. Life is too intriguing. Though every being has a purpose of his or her life, but it is very difficult to find the purpose of the life. Only God knows the purpose of one's life. One's life journey is always according to his or her life purpose for that given journey of life. Spirituality is the way of getting success and finding peace in the life. Managing the mind is the purpose of life. Being happy in the life is the purpose of life. Experiencing the life is the purpose of life. Unconditional love and its indiscriminate spread among all is the purpose of life. Doing good karma, i.e. thinking and acting good, is the purpose of the life. Positive thinking is the purpose of life. To remain stable in every situation of life, and then aptly responding to the situations of life, is the purpose of life. Exhibiting best human traits is the purpose of life. Loving the whole creation and the creator is the purpose of life. State of being happy or being sad is just a creation of the mind. Nothing is for real in this life. Creations in the life are the creations of mind. The purpose of the life is to manage the mind in the favour of the life. Mind has memories. Eliminate bad memories. Do Dhyana or meditation or yoga, and come to know about the purpose of life. Getting enlightened and awakened is the purpose of life. Life is inside the being and not outside. Death is outside the being. Make the mind thoughtless, i.e. free of thoughts. Life is at its best, when the mind is at rest. Escape from fears is not the solution, but face the fears. If once faced, fears will go away for good. Life itself is the biggest purpose. Dying a meaningful, peaceful and blissful death is the purpose of life. Therefore, there is not one purpose of the life, but from birth till death, and also, beyond the death and before the birth, all that happens to the life, is the purpose of life. The purpose of life is life.

CHAPTER SEVEN

Positive Attitude

Attitude defines the life of a being. Attitude affects the karma, and karma creates destiny. Attitude makes a big difference in the life. A right attitude and needed ability are necessary for getting success in anything in the life. A right positive attitude brings excellence in works and actions. Attitude is the attire of a being, which is always carried by him or her from birth up to death, and also beyond, in the form and shape of tendencies of the mind (subconscious and unconscious mind) in the afterlife, in the spirit form, in the Spirit World. Attitude of a being is reflected in his or her thinking, and his or her thinking patterns are moulded accordingly. Positive thinking is an outcome of positive attitude. Attitude is the way one thinks, feels or behaves. Thoughts affect the life through actions. Overcome and allay fears and anger. One's attitude is one's persona and his or her personality. Personality is the quality of having a strong, interesting and attractive character. Personality of a being makes him or her different from other beings. Have right attitude in the life, and also, towards the life. Have right and positive attitude for self, and for every other thing. A right attitude, takes a being away from fears, to full and absolute freedom. Profoundness of life cannot be understood without having a right positive attitude.

Thinking affects the life, and makes it according to itself. Attitude should be such that it annihilates all pressures and tensions in the life. Imagine life free from all tensions and worries. It is all possible by having a right perspective about the life. Attitude creates perspective. Life is all about the right perspective. Attitude and perception also, affect each other. Attitude should not be suppressing and repressive, as it may stop the opportunities from coming into being's life. Positive thinking brings desired changes in one's behaviour and the attitude. A right attitude changes the nature of problem in one's life, and gives him or her enough strength, to solve the problem. Life is a prison. Right positive attitude helps a being to come out of this prison and break all shackles. Life is set of problems. Had problems been not there, there would have been no life either. Life is a test. Physical plane (earth) is a training school. Every problem in life is essentially an experience of the life. Life is given by the God for experiencing it, working over it, and thereby, advancing the soul. Look at the celebrities and other successful beings. Along with much hard work in a direction, it is their correct attitude, which takes them to the greater heights and booming success in physical domain. Become less concerned about the future, and live in the present. This attitude towards the life will keep one away from all unwanted and undesirable stresses, pressures and tensions in the life. Freedom is life. Worry is death. We attract the energy, which is given out to something. Give energy to happiness and joy, and the happiness and the joy will return. If energy is given to worries, worries will only return. We all are our own creators, i.e. our own gods. It is the Law of Attraction. We attract, what we think. Affirm positivity to self. Affirmations are powerful. Affirmations are emotional supports and encouragement. Affirmations go into the mind. Affirm mind with positive statements. Body follows the thought process. We become what only we believe, and what others believe about us, should not and does not matter and affect us. Manage the mind. Positive thinking is an outcome of proper mind management, which creates positive attitude in beings.

CHAPTER EIGHT

Right Thinking

Always think right, no matter what. One's thoughts in the mind, create one's spoken words. Thoughts affect the quality of life, and its every related aspect. Thoughts radiate vibrations and energy. Thoughts travel and reach every corner of the universe. Right thinking is, "think before thinking". Thoughts and thinking create karma. Manage the mind. As, karma creates destiny, therefore, thoughts create destiny. What one sows, one reaps. Thing sent, is only returned. It is the law of the universe. Goodness sent, returns as help, good fortune, situations and circumstances in one's life. Life is a continuous journey. What happens to one in this life, is the result of karma of present life, or of the previous life(s). One's destiny is, his or her own creation. God is never discriminatory in giving good life to one being, and the bad life to the other being. One's life is one's own making. If mind is not managed, and thoughts and actions are not changed, then, same patterns will return again and again in one's life. Be nice to everybody in the life, without caring for his or her thoughts and actions. Stay good, even if, others are behaving badly. One's past becomes one's present, and one's present will eventually become one's future. Never be resentful, critical and judgemental, in order to create good karma in the present times, and the present journey of life. We all are energies. Radiate good energies. Good energy is created by good thoughts and good actions. Our life situations, external environment and its factors, are the energies, which are present internally and also externally, which are created by the self, and also, by the others in the surroundings or the environment. Consciousness is energy. One's true identity is one's soul or the spirit, and not the physical or the gross body. How others behave with us, is our karmic account with them. We all meet each other many times in this infinite journey of life, so we create karmic accounts with each other. It is the karmic account, which creates this trap of birth-death-rebirth. Be nice with even those, who have harmed, as it is going to help you only. By doing so, new karmic account will not be created. Forgive others for their bad behaviours, and forget bad memories, bad situations and the bad circumstances of the life. Be fearless in the life, but greatly fear of doing any bad karma. One always wears his or her samskara (संस्कार), and the karma, in every journey of life. Meditation and Yoga create right thinking. Energies exchanged, must be smooth and positive, and not turbulent. Life is beautiful. We create its beauty, and nobody else. Bless self, before blessing others. Right thinking is a blessing for self, and also, for the others. Empower the soul, and heal the spirit. We all have a divine flame inside. "I am an angel", sent by the God, say it to self, consciously, and do its self-talk, in order to remain light in the journey of life. Right thinking is created by a powerful and a peaceful soul, and the vice versa.

CHAPTER NINE

Positive Thinking

Contacts of sense objects, i.e. organs of touch, sight, hearing, smell and taste, with the phenomena, create perceptions. Positive thinking urges and continuously inspires one to keep putting efforts towards the goals and desires of life. Never stop your efforts and actions. Do not care or worry for the outcomes. For every input, there is an output. It is the law of universe. The nature of outcomes will be as per the design of the life, already scripted by the God. A being should give his or her best possible performance in every situation. Positive thinking mitigates the effects of bad luck or negativity in the life. Positive thinking suppresses negative thinking. Negative thinking always leads to failures, miseries and discontentment in the life. Negative thoughts never yield positive results or positive outcomes. Expect positive results and positive outcomes in the life. It is positive thinking. Positive thinking leads to good, reliable and dependable relationships in the life. Always help others. Have realistic expectations in the life, from self and the others. Identify strengths and weaknesses. Expectations should match with the strengths. Thinking may be wishful and unrealistic, and such thinking will never pay in the life. Positive thinking makes one to, feel the freedom of life, and live in the present moment. Positive thinking is too contagious and infectious spreads happiness and keeps the beings away from worries. Think about the achievements, and not about the obstacles and the problems. Make positive thinking, conation of life. Positive thinking is positive life. Thoughts change the experiences of life. Positive thinking is the fountainhead of energy, which is needed for a happy life. Learn to handle the thoughts. Thoughts have ability to create heaven or hell in the life. What one thinks, definitely manifests in his or her life. What is being repeatedly thought of, one becomes exactly like that. Life should be great and big, no matter what. Thoughts are very powerful. Thoughts mould one's personality. Thoughts become the realities of life. Positive thinking creates miracles in the life. Meditation, Yoga and deep breathing help in positive thinking. Positive thinking radiates. Practise positive thinking consciously. For positive thinking, never brood, regret, nag or dwell on something which is unpleasant. Use proper words in self-talk. Self-talk is an internal dialogue. Become an optimist, for which self-talk must be full of hopes and positive. Positive thinking must be lived. Attitude is everything in life. Positive thinking is an outcome of positive attitude. One's beliefs make his or her life. Be appreciative towards, and thankful to, everything in the life. In this cosmos, miracles are taking place everywhere every time, just sharpen the senses to experience these. God is there sitting inside every creation in this show of life. Pay salutation to everything in the nature. Look for positive in everything, and go through the life, with positive attitude. Have attitude of gratitude. Difficulties are part of the life, but with the help of positive thinking, no difficulty remains a difficulty. Problems of life are tests of life. Problems are the pointers of the presence of the God in one's life, and evince God's direct involvement or communication with that being. Problems make life colourful, if dealt with successfully, with the right attitude and the positive thinking, while using one's full potential and all abilities. Cultivate the mind. Overcome compulsive emotional patterns. Protect energies. Focus on the mind. Make the God, a partner in everything you do in your life. Overcome negative thinking. Remember, thinking decides one's destiny of life, so choice is all yours.

CHAPTER TEN

Positive Thinking And Optimism

Optimism and the hope are the key elements of the life. Optimism is the feeling that future of being will be good and successful. Optimism is about having the faith in the God. Optimism is a form of positive thinking. Optimism is essentially the belief, in the self. Optimism is, believing that being is only responsible for happiness in his or her life. Optimism is all about the faith and convincing the self that, good things will continue happening in life. What we think, ultimately we become. Things thought repeatedly start happening in the life. One's subconscious mind starts working on that thought in order to manifest that thing, with all the help from the universe, in being's life. Law of Attraction works, and the things wished for, start getting attracted in one's life. Experiences of the life and the world are essentially the creations of mind. Therefore, work on the mind, in order to create the kind of life, which is wished for. Optimism is a thought, imbued with the mind. Optimism is the nectar of the life, and pessimism is the poison of the life. Optimism is not just a mindset, but the behaviour. Optimism gives courage to beings. Optimism is quite essential to all the achievements in the life. An optimist always learns from his or her mistakes and failures. An optimist always believes that something wonderful is going to happen in his or her life. Ways to become an optimist are, focussing on the success and only the positive sides of the problems, situations and circumstances, identifying a role model, keeping a gratitude journal, and challenging and changing the arising negative thoughts. Positive thinking and optimism are interlaced with one another. Optimism instils required confidence in a being to win over another being or a difficult situation of life. When a being is filled with positive thoughts and optimism, mind generates many options of solving the problem. Life has no set path. All the paths have their own beauty. Life is a continuous journey.

CHAPTER ELEVEN

Mindset For Positive Thinking

Mindset is the general attitude of a being and his or her fixed ideas, which are very often quite difficult to change. Overconfidence and underconfidence both are bad, and lead to failures in the life. Confidence is a cognitive bias. Confidence is characterized by an estimation of, one's ability to perform, or his or her performance relative to that of the others. Have no expectations, if possible, in order to remain happy in the life. Understand the difference between the realities and imaginations. Remove all fears and anxieties. Make full efforts after correct and realistic thinking. A positive mindset is necessary for achieving the set realistic and visualised goals in the life. Imagine the ways, you wish your life to be, after certain time durations, one after the other, in the life. Mindset is mind's thought process. Life is all about a correct mind's thought process. Create a mindset, which brings happiness and joy in the life. Between yesterday's mistakes and tomorrow's hope, there is an opportunity for creating a right thought and performing in the right direction today. It is always a fantastic opportunity in every being's life. Live in today. Love the present moment and today. A winning mindset is created by putting self in the challenging new situations, finding a mentor in the life, accompanying bright talented and successful beings, eliminating stress, taking every failure as a learning opportunity and keeping a journal of proudest moments of the life. A change of the mindset, along with it, changes everything inside and outside of a being. Mindset changes one's world and the experiences of the life. Change in the mindset, changes the problem or its nature. Mind and the mindset are everything. Eliminate the mindset of "I cannot" with "I can". Success is an outcome of positive mindset and positive thinking. Failure is an outcome of negative mindset and negative thinking. Challenges in the life are the opportunities for testing the current mindset, and correcting it to the next level. Life is good as per the goodness of the mindset. A right mindset, always enthuses and encourages a being. Failing to try is simply trying to fail. Do meditation and yoga for a right and a winning mindset. Connect with the nature and the God, for a right mindset. A right mindset always creates a positive thinking.

CHAPTER TWELVE

Goals and Desires

Do right goals setting, and also, set correct and achievable realistic targets in the life. Goal(s) setting, spurs positive and right thinking, and also, motivates one to do inordinate hard work for achieving the goal(s). Actions must be in the direction of achieving the goal(s), so set. Give 100%, through actions. Limited desires must be there in the life. More desires may simply disturb the peace of mind. First deserve, and then, desire. Goals and desires are not the life. The life is all about correct thinking and correct actions. Goals and desires should be such that these bring peace, love and happiness in the life. Life is too small to celebrate, but too long to live. A being must decide between celebrating and living, as regards the life. Have firm belief in self. Self-confidence is quite necessary for achieving the set realistic goals of the life. But, alone, self-confidence is not enough, as it also needs ability. Life is limitless, replete with magic and miracles, and full of all possibilities. There is nothing more magical than the life itself, in this entire creation. Do not limit life's possibilities. When one door of happiness closes in the life, another door opens. Life is tested, not by the success in the life, but by the ways of handling the problems and failures in the life. A pat is also good in the life, and a slap is also good in the life.

Always be happy in the life. Splash the life perfectly with colours of hard work and success. Life is infinite, but each journey of life is too short, and passes too quickly. Laugh, love and try new things in the life. Experience the life. Forgive, forget and do no hold any grudges in the life. One needs strength, while doing the possible things in the life, whereas, he or she needs faith, while doing the impossible things, in the life. Never stop trying. Satisfaction lies in making all possible efforts, and not in the attainment(s). Full efforts made, is full victory. Winning without risk(s), is triumph without glory. One cannot climb a mountain without risking a fall. Both the situations of success or failure are good, because if one wins, then he or she can lead, but if, he or she loses, then he or she can guide. Be innovative, and also, an explorer. Eliminate confusions in the life through discussions, in order to reach and arrive at the solutions. Be great in the life. The desire to succeed and the urge to reach full potential are the keys for unlocking the door to personal excellence. A stumble always does not create a fall, but at times, also prevents a fall. Invisible forces accompany every being throughout his or her journey of life, and help him or her, at every stage of the journey of life. Be conscious and aware enough to sense-perceive, and receive that help. There is always a help for a yelp, in this God's creation. All successful beings are positive thinkers, and they have two things, viz. definite goals, and burning desires to achieve these goals.

CHAPTER THIRTEEN

Positive Thinking And Stress Elimination

Stress is a state of mind, a feeling, feeling of emotional or physical tension. Stress makes one to feel frustrated or angry or nervous. Stress is body's reaction, reaction to a change or a challenge or a demand. Laugh and smile, as these reduce the stress, and act as antidepressants. Stress is always not negative, but many times it is positive also, as it helps one avoiding a danger, or meeting a deadline. Stress and anxiety both, are the states of the mind, and create a state of unrest and unease. Stress can be eliminated by, positive thinking, mindfulness meditation, displaying appreciation and showing gratitude, doing yoga, tai chi, and qigong, doing physical exercises, playing a sport, lighting a candle, chewing gum, hobnobbing with great and good beings, considering supplements, reducing caffeine intake, laughing and spending quality time, breath focussing (long, slow, deep breaths, known as abdominal or belly breathing), using guided imagery and repeating a prayer. Control the thoughts. Do not manage the stress, but eliminate it. Cultivate extreme resilience. Stress is a trap created by the mind. Majority of beings are trapped in such psychological games created and played by their minds.

Increase self-love. Self-love is a state of appreciation for oneself. Self-love grows from self-actions, which support one's physical, psychological and spiritual growth. Self-love is having a high regard for your own well-being, and the happiness. Self-love is taking care of your own needs. Self-love is not sacrificing self-well-being in order to please the others. Entire life is an endless quest of "to control", which simply creates stress. Interestingly control in the life, is a myth. What is perceived as control, is mere an illusion of control. Set goals are the source of this illusion of control. “I have control”, is the illusion of control. A being must recognise the emotional domain, which he or she occupies, as it will help him or her in the mind management, thus, leading to positive thinking and eliminating the stresses in his or her life. Eliminate mental chatters and create a right mental model. Do not label the events of life as either good or bad. In the life, whatever happens, beyond the realm of control, is not bad. It is just an event of the life. Emotional energy should not be squandered. Invest more in the process, and not in the outcome(s). It is the mantra of a happy life, with no stresses, and in essence, it is the outcome of positive thinking.

CHAPTER FOURTEEN

Positive Thinking And Happiness

Happiness is a feeling of pleasure and positivity. Happiness arises from positive thinking. Happiness is the very purpose of life. Happy beings are very creative. Envision a great life, great happiness, and the happiness will come. Attract happiness. It is the power of thinking, essentially the power of the mind. Happiness is a sense of well-being, joy, excitement and the contentment. Happiness brings smile. Happiness is the feeling that comes over a being, when he or she knows that his or her life is good. When beings are successful or safe or lucky, then they feel happiness. Happiness is the characteristic of the soul. Happiness is relaxing and healing in nature. When beings feel good, proud, excited, relieved or satisfied about something, then, they become happy. Happiness is the measure of life's success. Happiness is prosperity. Happiness is joy, contentment and enjoyment. Happiness is glee, delight, optimism and euphoria. Happiness is elation and exhilaration. Happiness in one's life comes by noticing, being active, giving, keep learning, and connecting. Happiness in one's life comes from his or her actions in the life. Happiness is well-being. Happiness is pleasure, jubilation, laughter and bliss. Happiness is gladness. Happiness is sanctity, joviality and cheerfulness. Happiness is playfulness. Happiness is the direct intervention and the presence of the God in one's life. Positive thinking and being receptive to new life experiences and ideas are simply interrelated. Happiness increases productivity. Pleasure, passion and purpose bring happiness in one's life. Joy is an emotion, an emotion evoked by one's well-being or success or good fortune, whereas, happiness is a state of the mind, a state of contentment or pleasure or satisfaction. Happiness is being brought into the life by, being resilient, being with others which make one to smile, imaging the best, finding purpose, accepting the good, holding on to values, listening to the heart, living in the present, pushing self and not the others, doing the things that one loves, managing the emotional, mental and physical energies, treating the self very well, being compassionate, and positive thinking. The God is the only source of positive thinking and happiness. Happiness is created in the mind. Manage the mind. The God is also the source of strength, hope, and the wisdom. The God is the creator of this entire creation. The God is the supreme energy. God is bliss. Therefore, believe in the God, in order to remain positive and happy in the life. Happiness is the gift in the life, given by the God. Being happy, is living in heaven. Being wretched, is living in hell. Heaven and hell are no two separate spaces or realms or domains or dimensions, but the two states of the mind. Happiness is the direction, the direction in the life to find the beauty in everything. Happy beings are the prettiest beings in this whole creation.

CHAPTER FIFTEEN

Training The Mind In Order To Stay Positive

Train the mind, in order to see good in everything in the life. Positivity is always a conscious choice. Happiness in the life is experienced and earned through practise, as it depends on the quality of one's thoughts. Eliminate all aleatory elements in the life through positive thinking and the mind management. The two choices in the life are, either to accept the conditions as they exist, or to accept the responsibility of changing these situations. We all are one, and also many, at the same time. Mind is everything. Life is nothing, but all about the mind management. Yoga and Meditation, do mind management. It is the mind, which controls the quality of life of a being. Mind thinks, and the brain calculates. Mind is non-physical. Mind is formless. Mind is an element of the consciousness. We become what we think. Mind orders and controls the brain and its operations. One's mind can become his or her best friend, or even the worst enemy. Therefore, train the mind well. Mind shapes the life. When in pain or distress or hurt, do not get discouraged, but use the mind well, as the life wants to teach and impress something on you. Life should not be taken as a possibility, but well understood as a game, through a well-trained mind, and the positive thinking. If mind is not controlled, then it will control the being. In the pursuit of peace and happiness in the life, learn to ignore. Ignore the bad, as it helps in staying positive. A good workout is also an effective way of clearing his or her mind of all negatives, and staying positive. Mind should be trained for success in the life. Ways to train the mind are, learning new things, doing meditation, relying on memory, reading much, trying puzzles, dancing, listening to good music, spending quality time, following hobbies and passions, learning a new skill daily, differentiating between ruminating and problem-solving, practising gratitude, being thankful, balancing the emotions through logic, practising spirituality, seeing the past lives and, autosuggesting yourself from time to time.

CHAPTER SIXTEEN

Eliminating Negative Thoughts

Identify self, and also, the life within, i.e. mind, body and the spirit. Life is not on the surface of the body, but inside in the body. Life is inside, and also, the outside of the physical or gross body. Life is God. Thoughts are created in the mind, and not in the brain. Mind thinks. Brain calculates. Explore the life. Destroy or annihilate any negative thought about, the self, others, the nature, world, or anything, when it is just beginning. Thought is weakest at the moment, when it is being created for the first time. Negative thought is a poison. Negative thoughts lead to the worst problems in the life. Nip the negative thoughts in the bud. A stitch in time saves nine. Let the problem of negative thoughts be sorted out immediately, as it may save a lot of extra efforts and works, which will be required to eliminate it later otherwise. Understand the life, and its dynamics, i.e. the life processes. The quality of thoughts must be consciously checked and evaluated. Mind listen to all thoughts, and acts in full obedience. Change samskaras and vibrations, if these are found to be negative. Samskaras or sanskaras (संस्कार) are one's mental impressions or recollections or psychological imprints. Never be critical or judgemental about the others. Negative thoughts mar the relationships in the life. Negative thoughts arise due to lack of their awareness and knowledge. Negative thoughts result in many physical ailments and diseases over the time, along with mental sickness. Regularly check the quality of thoughts. Never transmit and receive bad or negative energy, but always transmit and receive good energy. Energy, which is given out, surely returns back. Law of Karma is the infallible law of universe. Law of Karma is the basis of whole creation. Even the incarnated great souls were not spared from the bad effects of their bad present karma and the bad past karmic accumulations. Negative thoughts spoil one's personality, and also, his or her performance. Live the life in the meditative style. Meditative state is the state of healing. Meditative state is reflective and deeply thoughtful state. When one reflects on his or her life, his or her important decisions and actions, then he or she is just meditative. Meditative state is the state of mind. One's energy field should always be high and strong enough, in order to, not to get negatively affected by others. One's thinking becomes his or her samskaras. Therefore, always think right and positive. Negative thoughts sap the soul of its power, whereas positive thinking empowers the soul. Do Yoga, Meditation and lots of physical exercises daily. Play sports. Eat and drink, good and well. Never get hurt by other's words, or be jealous, or become angry, and never criticise, but always be appreciative. It is positivity. Practise to stop and replace the negative thoughts, by thoughts audit, and practising the art of positive thinking. Do positive mind self-talk. Mind cannot be made to do anything forcefully, as it does that thing more and more, which it is told, not to do. Mind can be managed only when, physiological processes (body) and psychological processes (mental) are considered in separation, and not in the unison. When "real me" and "my mind" are separated, and then worked upon in the direction of elimination of negative thinking, then the negative thoughts are not just avoided for some time, but are finished / eliminated for good.

CHAPTER SEVENTEEN

Power Of Positive Thinking

Dwell on positive thinking only. Radiate positive thinking. Positive thinking is quite powerful, and it furthers one's mental agility. Thinking affects the life. It affects one's physical, mental and emotional health. Positive thinking cultivates inner resilience in a being. Positive thinking further sharpens and makes the power of mind more intense. Stay positive in order to remain happy in the life. Free yourself from all stresses. Connect with the nature. Nature is not different from us, or we are not different from the nature, but one and the same. Use affirmations for positive mind, happiness and wealth in the life. Negativity and worrying, damage the body, mind and the spirit. Positive thinking rejuvenates and revitalises every cell of the body. Cell is the memory house of a being. Cell is affected by the mind and the consciousness. Cell affects the material body. Cell is responsible for the state of the physical health and stability of a being. Remove unkindness and melancholy. Cell is the kernel of the physical or gross body. Do not pass just a mundane life, but live an excited life, always ignited, and kindling with love and kindness. Thought affects the cell(s). Thought is everything. Mind creates thoughts. Thought is associated with an emotion and a feeling. Mind travels from one life journey to another life journey. Nature of mind is je ne sais quoi. Mind through the cells affects and controls internal releases, secretions and hormonal discharges. Every cell is affected by every thought. Life is manifestation of thoughts. Thoughts create realities in the life. Live a simple and ordinary life with extraordinary thoughts and actions. Be straight to yourself. Do not try to prove, what you are not. Positive thinking is necessary for spiritual growth and evolution. Good thoughts lead to good actions, and the bad thoughts lead to bad actions. Overcome compulsive emotional patterns through mind management by using the power of positive thinking. Circumstances in the life have been well orchestrated by the nature and the God for being's spiritual growth and overall well-being. Experiencing repeats itself in the life, till the needed change does not occur in the being. Life is a teacher. Nature is also a teacher. Life is a learning opportunity. Enhance the quality of thoughts. Cultivate noble and sublime thoughts. Fill life with inspiration and purposes. Life lived is an effect, with definite causes. This universe is not a chaos, but a well ordered whole, with cause(s) and effect(s). Many causes are controllable, and yet, many others are just uncontrollable. Put mind for productive purposes. Thoughts bring happiness or wretchedness. Thoughts attract similar situations and circumstances in the life. Positive thinking brings positive energy, and thus, enthuses a being. Visualise yourself as a lovely and a powerful soul of the God, and thus, instil yourself with positivity and energy. Optimism, hope, belief, faith and right attitude are the outcomes of positive thinking. Attitude and aptitude determine the altitude gained in the life. Success is a state of mind, brought forth by the positive thinking. Be thankful in the life. Your life is not just your creation, but contributions by all, and the visible and the invisible forces of the universe. Be thankful to the God, and all the spirits around. God makes all necessary arrangements in the life without any exception and discrimination. Human form of life has a free will option, whereas other life forms do not have it. Therefore, human beings, through right, will, choices and decisions, i.e. right karma (right thought and right action), can create a better fortune, fate and the destiny for themselves, which other species and life forms cannot. Positive thinking must always be followed by positive doing. A negative mind, can never give any being, a positive life. Positive thinking is all powerful. Challenging situations and the obstacles are the part of the life. Focus, only on the good things in the life. Practise gratitude. Do not be po-faced, but open yourself up to humour. Accompany positive people for positive thinking, and thus, creating and leading a meaningful life. Practise positive self-talk. Identify negative areas, and work on them, so as to eliminate them. Start and end, every single day of the life on a positive note with smile on the face, and peace in the mind.

CHAPTER EIGHTEEN

Positive Thinking And Good Health

Life has many ways to live it, and to love it. Positive thinking leads to the good health. Positive thinking holistically comprises all possible ways of life, of living it, and also, loving it. Health is the condition of a being's body and the mind. Good health brings stability (emotional, mental and physical) in the life. Good health is the sense of wholeness within the self. Every being is made up of body, mind and the spirit. Body must be vibrant. The three health elements in every being are mental health, emotional health and physical health. Emotions must be exuberant. This body is matter (physical), which is the temple or residence of spirit (non-physical). Soul lives inside the body. Soul loves the body. It is the reason of being's fear of death. Therefore, every being must take full care of his or her body. Positive mind creates positive thoughts. Mind must be peaceful and joyful always. Mind is responsible for the all three health, viz. mental health, emotional health and the physical health. Use mind properly in life, for well-being of self, and also, of the others. Goodness and wellness start with the self. Health is the greatest wealth, and also, the true richness of life. Happiness is the highest form of good health, and enthusiasm is the indicator of good health. Eat good and right kind of food for the body like consume honey or eat ash gourd, and also, have good and positive thoughts in the mind. Right food enhances one's mental capability and mental stability. Only a body in good health can have a clear and a strong mind. Health of the body is essentially the health of every cell in the body. Therefore, health is subtle and micro, manifesting itself at the macro level. Keep body energies in good, state and amount. Intellect needs energy. Emotions need energy. Give expression to the emotions. Physical actions need energy. Exert the body. Sweat profusely as a result of great physical exertion. Empty the colon completely after getting awake, early in the morning. Keep colon clean and purged. Do yoga and meditation, and play sports. Good physical health is essential in the life. Meditation is must for health and healing. Have positive thoughts, and perform good actions only. Health is the greatest possession, which a being can have in his or her life. Good health brings hope in the life, and the hope is everything. Health is physical, as well as spiritual. Health is physiological and psychological in its nature. Use affirmations for a perfect health. One must be physically and psychologically fit, in order to enjoy the life, and to live it fully. Listen to the good healing music. See, the lights of nature, the rising sun, the setting sun, its shimmering reflections on the water, waves of water of sea, majestic mountains, peaceful deserts, the clouds and the sky, the dancing plants due to the wind, the blooming flowers, the flying birds and butterflies, the frolicking squirrels, the dancing peacock, prancing kangaroos, the colourful rainbow, the falling rain, shoals of fishes, pride of lions, gaggle of geese, and listen to the sound of the blowing wind and the rattling leaves and sprigs, feel the soft touch of rain drops. It is all the magic of nature, spreading all over, hold it. Connect with the nature and all its elements like fire, water, light, soil etc.. It is the nature only, which supports, manages and balances a being's life. Indulge in hobbies and passions. Do the things passionately in the life at every moment. Nobody can ever die of hunger; as otherwise, it puts a big question mark on the design of universe and the nature, and the existence of the God. A being dies due to his or her terrible actions. We create our own destiny. Death must be graceful and not miserable, and must be celebrated like birth no matter what. Every being is born with some talent. Every being is not made for everything, but definitely for something. Every being and every entity in this creation is just unique, magical and very special in itself. Honour and respect every other thing. Doing so, is paying respect and showing reverence to the God and his creation. Reverence is a feeling of profound awe and respect accompanied with great love. Control the ego, because ego controls the life. For wellness, work on body, mind, emotions and the energy, and manage these rightly. Balance the energies within. Live the life in complete exuberance and effervescence. Positive thinking has a direct bearing on physical and mental goodness.

CHAPTER NINETEEN

Power Of Positive Affirmations

Affirmations greatly work, and these are one of the big secrets of the life, and the universe. Every thought and every spoken word is an affirmation. Begin to consciously create the life, the way it is being envisioned, which pleases and supports, by using the power of positive affirmations. Have a gratifying and a fulfilling journey of life. Release all limitations. Self-talk and internal dialogues are the streams of affirmations. Thoughts and beliefs are the biggest tools to change the course of life. Positive affirmations bring positive changes in the life, and raise the confidence and the self-esteem. Positive affirmations work on the mind, and eliminate all negative thoughts, and also, other destructive patterns, and bring in positive thinking. Positive affirmations also release a being from all his or her fears, worries and anxiety. Affirmations should be repeated over and over again. Gradually and imperceptibly, affirmations begin to take charge of thoughts, actions and the mind. Affirmations change the pattern of thinking. Affirmations change the life. Positive thoughts and words create good experiences in the life. Retrain thinking and speaking, if these are not positive, into the positive patterns, in order to improve the quality of life. Affirmations open up the secrets doors of the universe for beings. Affirmations work on the subconscious mind, and use the power of the subconscious mind, in order to change the life. Affirmations are being used every moment, whether one knows about these or not. One affirms and creates his or her life experiences with his or her every word and thought. Beliefs are habitual thinking patterns. Some of the created beliefs are too supportive, but many other beliefs might be too destructive, and thus, greatly limit one's ability to adapt or adopt or create the things said or wanted in the life. Thoughts are the impediments between one's wish, and the belief of being suitable for it. Therefore, there is a need to pay attention towards the thoughts. Learn how to think and talk. Eliminate all such thoughts, which create the experiences that one does not want in his or her life, e.g. complaints. Every time, when one gets angry, he or she is reaffirming that he or she wants more and more anger in his or her life. Every time, when one feels like a victim, he or she is reaffirming that he or she wants to continue to feel like a victim. Therefore, change the thinking, and the type and level of talks. A persistent feeling of life being cruel will really never make the life beautiful. What we think, we become. Thoughts create experiences in the life. Be goody-goody. Some of the affirmations, which one must tell to him or herself every single day are, I am doing the best and it will come, I love myself, I create my own success and happiness, I am responsible for my life, I believe in my dreams and I am grateful for every day of my life. Interestingly, a being wants everything permanent for his or her, this temporary stay on earth. Affirmations bring positive changes in health, relationships, finance and every other aspect of the life. Saying anything is affirmation in itself, so never say anything, which is negative or discouraging. Affirmations, which are said multiples times with great feelings, manifest early in the life. Actions are affirmations. Therefore, do good acts, for attracting good things in the life. Affirmations are like the seeds, put into the soil. For affirmations to work quickly, and also consistently, prepare a proper atmosphere, as a seed to grow, needs proper nutrition, water and the sun. It is the secret of affirmations to work in the life. Good and happy thoughts make affirmation to work faster. One's thoughts are his or her matter of choice, so create right and correct thoughts. Choose to change the thinking, and make it positive. Always feel good. Speak the affirmations out loud for some time; say for about five minutes, and three or four times a day. Look at yourself in the mirror, and then repeat the positive statements. Power of affirmations builds the power of the mind. Some other affirmations are, I embrace the rhythm of life, I can become anything, I shall do hard work, and My intuition always works and takes me in the right direction. Affirmations work better during sleep, and the statements and words are deeply impressed into subconscious mind in sleep. During sleep, conscious mind is switched off, therefore, words and messages enter very easily into the subconscious mind without any resistance of the conscious mind. Affirmations are powerful, and make what one is today, and what he or she wants to become tomorrow.

CHAPTER TWENTY

Law Of Attraction

What one thinks, he or she becomes. What one feels, he or she attracts. And, what one imagines, he or she creates. This is the mantra of successful and happy life. Start living the life, which is envisioned. Law of Attraction uses the powers of the mind, and the powers of the universe. Mind and the universe are not isolated and separate, but essentially well connected, rather integrated. Whole creation is one and the same, i.e. just another you, and the creator and the creation are not separate and disjointed, but intermingled and integrated. A bird or a plant or a rock is not different and distinct from a human being, but one and the same, just having another form (shape and size). This whole universe, works on a common universal consciousness, and everything affects every other thing in the universe. Planets affect us, and we affect the planets. Nature affects us, and we affect the nature. This common universal consciousness is sort of average of all individual consciousness of every individual creation. The source of all consciousness in this creation is one, which is supreme consciousness, known as the God. Thus, the source of everything as sense-perceived is one and the same. Therefore, we all are connected through our consciousness. Consciousness is energy. My intentions affect the others, and theirs affects me. Here, "other" includes every other thing in the creation, other than me. There is no exclusivity and discrimination in the nature, but all-inclusivity and, equality and equity. Never ever question, the acts of nature. Never ever question or doubt the existence of the God. God is the energy running this whole creation, the whole show of life. We all are energies, individuated from the God, the supreme energy. Do introspection and check intents, thoughts and the actions. Nature acts on the commands of the God. Nature never reacts, but always responds in the best possible favourable ways. Nature tries to restore the equilibrium through its acts. It is the Law of Equilibrium. Law of Karma helps in the execution of the Law of Equilibrium. Nature is never hostile, but always friendly. Life is always on the mercy of the nature. Nature is too supportive always. Nature is our best friend. Positive thinking attracts the positive things in the life. Law of Attraction works always. We all send out, and also, receive the energy(s), continuously during the entire journey of life. Be the energy, which is to be attracted. Imagine living in the abundance, and abundance will be attracted in the life. Three pedestals of Law of Attraction are faith, belief and patience. The Law of Attraction simply states that positive thoughts bring positive results in the life, while negative thoughts bring negative results in the life. Thoughts are a form of energy. It is the positive energy, which attracts success in all areas of life, viz. health, finances, relationships etc.. Nature abhors vacuum. Remove negative things from the life in order to create space for the positive things. Like attracts like. Similar things are attracted to one another. Present is always perfect. Use positive affirmations. Affirmations are quite powerful. Identify negative thinking and eliminate it. Work on the mind and create positive thinking. Positive thinking is quite powerful, and brings in, the desired changes in the life. Be thankful and grateful. Always look at the positive in every situation. Learn to convert the negative into the positive. And, visualise the goals set in the life. Law of Attraction will then work for you.

CHAPTER TWENTY-ONE

How To Begin A Day

Life must be healthful. Life is very precious. Get awake at 3.40 AM. Immediately after getting awake, roll to the right side, and then get up from the bed. Doing so is too beneficial physiologically for heart and circulation of blood throughout the body. The first thing to be done after getting awake is to smile. Every single day of the journey of life of a being, begins with certain conditions, and brings in some challenges. Start every day of the journey of life, on a good and a very pleasant note. Mind is at maximum peace early in the morning. Sleep is a natural meditation. Sleep has healing effects on the body, mind and the spirit. Sync among the body, mind and spirit must remain established. A loss of it is the cause of many ailments in the beings. Yoga brings this sync, and helps it to remain established in the beings. Energy is filled into the body in morning by the universe. Freshness pervades all over in the nature, and the surroundings of a being. Whole creation sings and dances in the morning. Resolve to do small things right. Small things are not really small, but actually big things in the life. It is the small which grows into big. Every journey of several miles starts with a first step taken for it, and it is made up of every single step. Be thankful to everything and to the God. Do prayers. Do spiritual practices in the morning. Do yoga and meditation. Yoga and meditation stop all the chatters of the mind. Yoga and meditation bring one into the rhythm with his or her life. Begin the day with gratitude. Gratitude is a very powerful emotion. It illuminates one's inside, and brightens up his or her outside. Resolve to bring richness and sweetness in all relationships in the life. Use positive affirmations for overall wellness. Resolve to do the things effectively and passionately. Resolve to give a best delivery of every task done. Good thoughts and positive thinking in the morning, affect the whole day. Every new morning in the journey of life is a new life, a new opportunity to enjoy and celebrate the life. Every new morning gives every being, a new lease on life. Every day of the life, is just another opportunity for one's renewed commitments towards everything in the life, renewed resolves, renewed determination, with renewed opportunities and chances, and thus converting the failures into the successes. Every new day brings an opportunity to create a new and a stronger bond of being with the nature and the universe. With every new day, a being gets further close to the death and to the God. Begin every day with a proper state of the mind. Get charged up with positivity, have a positive vision, look at the positive side and deal with the negative side, in the morning. Peace and joy are the real riches and the assets of life. Accept whatever comes your way, even if it is unpleasant, if it is uncontrollable. It is the God's plan, and only a small portion of the bigger picture. Decide to help others at the beginning of the day. Thoughts travel, and come back in the form of experiences in the life. Resolve to invest good energy every morning, i.e. the energy of love, energy of kindness, energy of empathy, and energy of sympathy. Being awake and wakeful is the life, whereas, sleep is the death. Practise wakefulness.

Wakefulness is a daily recurring brain state, and also, the state of one's consciousness. In the wakeful state, a being is conscious and aware. And, he or she engages in active and coherent cognitive and behavioural responses to the external world. To start a day right, one must do physical exercises, drink suitable quantity of water, go outside in sun, make plans and the stick to the schedules, set the mindset, laugh, express love and think positive.

CHAPTER TWENTY-TWO

Meditation

Meditation is a definite state, and it involves use of technique(s) like focussing, mindfulness etc.. Meditation is focusing the mind on a particular object or a thought, or just on an activity. Meditation sharpens the levels of attention and the awareness of beings. Meditation helps in achieving a mentally clear, emotionally calm and a stable state. A being must become "meditation", as meditation is not done. Meditation is a certain state, a certain quality, i.e. a state of best sync among the mind, body and the spirit. Meditation must blossom within. Meditation is a spiritual diet for mind, body and the spirit. Meditation promotes overall health of beings. Meditation greatly helps in staying positive with the help of positive thinking. For a happy and wealthy life, give sufficient time in the life, for prayers, meditation and reflection. Meditation brings peace of mind, and therefore, peace in one's life. A meditative being never dies. Meditation eliminates the fear of death. Meditation also eliminates all other fears of life, like fear of getting old, failure, loss in the business, loss of the job, anxieties, anger, depression and insecurities. Meditation nourishes and blossoms the divinity within. Meditation brings wisdom. Wisdom in turn brings hope, happiness and joy, success, understanding, and most importantly, peace in the life. Everything is a thought. Thought is energy. Meditation works on mind and the thought(s). Meditation and Yoga are the best medicines to cure any ailment or a disease related to the body and the mind. Anything, which brings peace of mind, and connects one with his or her higher self or real self is meditation. Listening to the music of choice or interest or liking, is a type of meditation. Dhyana is not exactly the meditation. Dhyana is a part of self-directed awareness process. Dhyana is contemplation, reflection and abstract meditation. Dhyana is one of the eight limbs of the classical Yoga. The eight limbs of Yoga are, Yama, Niyama, Asana, Pranayama, Pratyahara, Dharana, Dhyana, and the Samadhi. Dhyana leads to self-absorption (Samadhi). Dhyana is a means of attaining Samadhi. Samadhi refers to the state of oneness, and the self-knowledge. One must cultivate his or her body, mind, emotion and energies to a level, in order to become "meditation". Do not become serious towards the life, instead become sincere towards the life. Meditation process involves focusing one's mind for a period of time, either in the silence or with the help of chanting. Various types of meditation processes are mindfulness meditation, mantra meditation, focussed meditation, progressive relaxation, movement meditation, loving-kindness meditation, spiritual meditation and the transcendental meditation.

CHAPTER TWENTY-THREE

How To End The Day

Living is a certain science. Living the life is an art. Go to sleep as per the demand of the body, and have a good quality of sleep. Sleep is a natural way of meditation. Sleep has healing effects on the body, mind and the spirit. Yogis take a sleep somewhere between 2 to 4 hours. As one grows religiously and spiritually, his or her hours of sleep go down. Eat a meal at least 3 to 4 hours before going to the bed. Drink certain amount of water before sleep, and use the affirmations. Digestion process must be over before one falls asleep. Sleep incubates one's thoughts. Therefore, it is better to have positive thoughts before going to sleep. There is a certain sleep science. Take a shower before going to the bed. Get some massage, if possible. Water is a magical element of the nature, and has the power to impress every cell of the body, and also the mind. Water has healing effects. Water affects the body externally when used externally, and the body and the mind internally when drunk. Water de-stresses a being and eliminates his or her anxieties. Do sleep sadhana. Sadhana means realisation. Sadhana is a spiritual exercise. In sadhana, the practitioner evokes the divinity, identifying and absorbing it into himself. Sadhana is the primary form of meditation. Every day of the life, at its end, adds to the life, some new wisdom and experiences. Finish or end the day on a good note. Do some meditation. Meditation reduces levels of stress, and boosts sleep hormone Melatonin. Make the mind peaceful. Forget the bad incidents of the day. Forgive all those, who had done something bad for you or misbehaved with you. Remember the God. Do bed time prayer before falling asleep. Remember that, which you wish to see in the dreams. Dream is astral travelling. Sleep is slipping into the death. One is never sure about next morning. Every new day in the journey of life is a rebirth of the being. While in sleep, the spirit of the being, wanders all over in this creation, visits the Spirit World, and also meets the God. Spirit is healed during the sleep of a being in the Spirit World. Sleep is a process. God blesses the spirit with new energy during the sleep. Getting suddenly awake either due to ringing of the alarm or due to any other reason is too dangerous, as it disturbs the sync among the body, mind and the spirit. Sleep is a paralytic state of the body. Body is predominantly made up of the matter, and takes some time to get active again. A sudden stimulus to body is never good. During sleep, the body and the spirit of a being are connected through a silver cord, and the spirit is out of the body. In trying to get or making suddenly awake, this silver cord connecting the body with the being's spirit through navel can get severed, leading to the death of being. Sleep has all physiological and psychological effects on the body. Light an organic lamp oil having a cotton wick in the house in the evening. Fire has ability to extirpate the negative energy of the house. Fire, water, air, sound, light are the powers of the nature, universe and the God. These simply improve the quality of life with their proper usage. Do some chanting before going to bed. Remind the self that I am not this body, before going to bed. Also, remind the self that I am not this mind either, before going to bed. If possible do some yogic practises, before going to the bed. Before going to the bed, read a book. Book reading drastically reduces the levels of stress. A nearly 6 minutes of reading reduces the stress by about 68%, as experienced. Feel the humidity before going to the bed, and keep the room dark. The best bed, which one can sleep on, is "peace and positivity".

CHAPTER TWENTY-FOUR

Music For Positive Thinking - Power Of Music

Music touches the life. Music is life. Music stimulates a range of emotions in beings. Life is a song, sing it well. Life is a beauty, praise it well. Sound is an existential pattern or the structure of the life. When words fail, then music speaks. Music is an expression of one's inner feelings, the experiences of the life and the definition of life. Music has certain geometry, a geometrical structure, and it involves mathematics. Music is one of the effective means of communication in the life. If you get tired in the journey of life, take rest, but do not quit, as quitting the journey of life will be a great disrespect of the God. Leave the past. Let past do not blackmail the present, and steal away the beautiful future ahead. Light and sound are two seminal creations in this existence, and rest, all further creations are their derivatives. Music is sound, with the light of divinity, as felt by the experiencer. There is music for every emotion in the life. Music is healing in nature. Music contains memories. Musical memories are preserved in the amygdala along with the feelings. Music appeals to the mind directly. Nature is source of music. Creation is an amalgamation of sounds. Winds, rain, clouds, waves of water, birds, trees, animals, all create sound. Sound is one of the powers of the nature, universe and the God. Music is a certain arrangement of available sounds, which is liked by the body, mind and the spirit. Noise is an unwanted arrangement of sounds. God loves music. The life likes and loves the beautiful harmonies as contained in a good music. Music has its own charm. Listening to good music is an astral traveling experience. Music becomes the carrier. Music is the diet of the soul. Music eliminates negativity, and initiates and props positive thinking in the beings. Music brings happiness and joy in the life. For every event in the life and the time, there is certain music. Music intends at connecting the creation with the creator. Music has the power to control the nature. Listen to the sounds of silence. Listen to the sounds of breath. There is a certain rhythm in it. It is the rhythm of the life within. If one key or note is lost, the whole rhythm is lost, and the life is lost. Creation is being recreated in the music by the musician. Music is an earnest prayer to the powers of the universe, which is heard by the God. Music travels the whole universe. Music has profound influence on the mind. Listen to the binaural beats and the isochoric tones. The word, "Aum (ॐ)" is a divine sound. Listen to a soulful music during meditation. Chants, prayers, mantra, all use the powers of the sound to reach the God. Music explores the geometrical patterns of the life, and also, of the whole creation. Sound or music, never dies, but reverberates in the universe for ever till eternity. Music has the ability to create all sorts of experiences in the life. Angels have a sound. Ghosts have a sound. The process of creation has a sound. The process of destruction also has a sound. Music with no spoken words into it is very affective and quite significant. Word is related to one's psychological structure. Music adds to the power of concentration and attention. Music cures diseases, and also, eases emotional, mental and physical pains. There is certain music for every act and every occasion in the life. Power of music is essentially the power of the positive thinking.

CHAPTER TWENTY-FIVE

Relationships And Positive Thinking

Relationships are the ways, beings feel about, or behave towards each other. Relationship is a friendly loving connection between beings. Relationship requires understanding, recognition, commitment, loyalty, love, patience and persistence. Life becomes a big mess, if one's relationships are not good in the life. Lucky is the being, which has good relationships with other beings, and also with the whole creation and the creator. Luck is created by human endeavours. To be lucky in the life is purely a matter of one's conscious choice(s). Being lucky is to be in the right state and the right position, at the right time, in the company of right kind of beings, and at the right place. In the journey of life, make a day of every day, and make a night of every night. Nature is a perfect mother, and it demonstrates right quantities of momism on the beings. Relationship is all about self-worth. It is all about being special to self and the others. A good relationship is based on positive thinking and rationality, and never lets one to feel alone in his or her journey of life. Relationship is about acceptance and forgiving, and forgetting the bad. Relationship is about holding the hand in the time(s) of need. Relationship is a constant companionship, and not just one time event. In good relationship(s), nobody is loser, but all are winners. Relationships are never perfect, but these are made perfect with the open minds. A real relationship maintains good relations through all ups and downs of the life. Maintaining relationship needs lots of substance of character. To transform a relationship, one needs to transform him or her first. Work hard to maintain the relations and relationships, as these are too fragile. All relationships are outcomes of the past or the present karma, and the exercise of free will, i.e. choices in the life. Free will is really not free. Good and bad, sense-perceptions, creation and destruction, all are the creation of one's mind. In whichever direction one wants to think, can think, because mind starts wandering that side. Some relationships are always sweet, whereas some other relationships remain sour throughout the life. Closest and permanent relationships are soul relations. Other relations are fake, false, and mere creation of the mind, which is based on selfish motives and improper understanding. There is no expectation, but complete selflessness in a real relationship. True relationship(s) is / are made in the Spirit World. One such relationship is the relationship between the mother and her child / children. Mother is the angel sent by the God on the physical plane, well before the child arrives on the physical plane (earth). However, both mother and children descend on the physical plane, and start and continue their journey of the life, only to pay off their karma, owed to one another. Breaking of a relationship is breaking of the understanding between the two beings. Give due time to the relationships, whether good or bad. Relationships need to be conducted on the daily basis. Relationships are never ever absolute in the case of life of beings, but keep varying always. Relationships need attention. Handling the relationships require certain skills. One's relationships with the God are always absolute. Relationship, as sense-perceived is a big illusion and lie of the life. It is an influence of Maya (the illusion causing cosmic element), and the mind. Relationship is about coming together. It is about caring and sharing. Relationship is not about extracting. In order to create, maintain and live a relationship, eliminate the negativity immediately. Only positive thinking can help create and then maintain true and good relationships. One's Samskara (संस्कार) determine his or her relationships with others. Samskaras or Sanskaras are one's mental impressions, recollections, and the psychological imprints. Eliminate expectations and comparisons, relationships will automatically improve. Work on the Samskara, which spoil or mar the relationships. Relationships must be sweet in order to have a happy journey of life. All good relationships in the life are based on the positive thinking only.

CHAPTER TWENTY-SIX

Behaviour At Workplace

Behaviour is the way, how one acts or behaves. Behaviour is always greater than the knowledge, and it reflects one's real education. One's behaviour is one's mirror, as it shows the being's real essence. Behaviour affects the relationships. Changed behaviour is always the best apology. One's behaviour at the workplace greatly affects his or her professional life, and also, the personal life and social life. Speak without offending any being. Similarly, listen without defending. One's social behaviour should be such that he or she is very easily approachable. One must understand the needs of other beings. A leader is not born by power, but by empowering others. A leader does not create followers, but creates more and more leaders. Effective teamwork begins and ends only with behaviour. One's work and the workplace, give meaning and purpose to him or her. Always carry a positive attitude at workplace. In order to understand the hearts and the minds of other beings, do not look at their achievements, but always look at their aspirations. One's job is his or her self-portrait; therefore, autograph the job with the excellence. Behaviour must be based on ethics, integrity, insight and inclusiveness. Success is measured by one's strength of desires and size of the dreams. Being boss is not just a job, but essentially a lifestyle. At workplace, one's actions must inspire others so as to dream more and more. Behaviour at the workplace must be based on positive thinking. A good leadership is always inspirational in its very nature. Extracting the greatness of the others is the greatness of a true leader or boss. An effective leadership is always based on clarity and the hope.

CHAPTER TWENTY-SEVEN

Behaviour At Home

Positive thinking positively affects one's behaviour. Children are the reasons for the life and the living, and also the love of the life, for their parents. Children are heart, soul and treasure of their parents. Sons quote their fathers in their words, and also, in their deeds. Mother's and daughter's love for each other, can never be separated. Daughters are like flowers and fill one's world and home with the beauty and the fragrance. Father is always, the superhero of the family. Father sets goals, dream and aspirations for his family. Father is reflection of God's care. Life comes with a mother. She is the angel sent by the God on the earth, before the children arrive. Motherhood is trait of willingness to include. Mother's love is a real peace, and the bliss in one's life. Grandparents make one's world softer, warmer and kinder. Grandparents love is stronger and deeper. Grandchildren fill the empty spaces of heart of the grandparents in the life. Grandchildren complete circle of love of one's life. A family is group of beings with intense karmic connections, ties and bonds with each other. Life begins with the family and the home. One's family is always a source of strength for him or her in the journey of life. Home is not just a place, but always a great feeling. A home is created by the beings that live together in a house. Homes shape one's course of life. Home creates memories of the life. Home is the residence of love. Be a role model by your good behaviour at home. Listen to all at home, actively and very carefully. Create a good environment at home by demonstrating good behaviour. Always keep promises. Raise yourself up or down to every being's level at the home. Choose your own battles. Express your feelings very frequently for others in the family. Catch your child being 'good'. Keep the things at home, as simple as possible, and always positive. Give the child, responsibility for his or her behaviour. Always maintain a sense of humour at home. Work on Samaskara. Encourage the members of the family to do prayers, meditation and yoga regularly. One's journey of life begins at home, and also, ends at the home. One's home must be the home of the God. Think and act positive, and make others in the family to do the same infallibly. Make your home, a heaven and worth life experience, for all of its members, with your good behaviour.

CHAPTER TWENTY-EIGHT

True Friends

One's true friends are his or her true asset of the life. Real friendship is the appetite of the soul. A sweet and real friendship is like a journey without an end. Friends are the siblings, which the God did not give. Friends are a family, which is chosen by the being. One gets his or her real friends in the journey of life due to his or her intense karmic connections with them. A best friend is like one soul in the two bodies. Friendship has a much greater impact on one's mental and physical health, and happiness. Mind works like a magnet. What it thinks, same is being attracted in the life. If one thinks of blessings, then blessings will be attracted in his or her life. If one thinks of problems, the problems will be attracted in his or her life. Therefore, it is necessary to cultivate good thoughts. Positive thoughts are good thoughts. Positive thoughts help one to stay positive and optimistic. One gets, what he or she thinks, and best deserves. Therefore, think positive, and thus, the life will automatically become positive. Good friends are attracted in the life, only by positive thinking. A true friend walks the talk. True friend shows that they really care, by their actions. True friends notice little things. True friends are dependable, and they always support. They act as a teacher and guide in one's life. True friends are self-sufficient. True friends are always good listeners, loyal, honest, non-judgemental and trustworthy. Friendship is one of the biggest blessings of the life, and a big gift to beings by the God. True friendship is the friendship of those beings, which are good and alike in their virtues. True Friend are quite loving, and caring and sharing. They make compromises. True friends believe in each other. They make time for each other, and remain respectful. They give more than they take. True friends forgive without an apology. Friends bring more happiness into the lives. True friends make one happy, contented and fulfilled in life. Healthy friendship elevates the mood, promotes overall growth, reduces stresses, and boosts outlook and the self-worth.

CHAPTER TWENTY-NINE

Positive Thinking And Performance

Positive thinking develops goal-orientation ability. Life of a being is not all that happens to him or her, but how he or she reacts to all these happenings. Reactions must be mature, and also, stable and positive. Convert reactions into the responses. Reactions lack rationality, whereas, responses carry substance and rationality. Positive thinking directly affects the performance of a being in his or her life. Always count your blessings in the life. Be thankful to the God for these blessings in the life. One's mentor, guru, family, relatives, neighbours and friends are the spiritual blessings in life, whereas his or her assets, wealth, job, promotions etc. are the physical blessings in life. Solve the problems of life, if these can be solved, else leave them, but do not live with the problems. Problems are the part of life's design, which is made uniquely for every being, as per the orders of the God. Challenges make life interesting, and overcoming them, make the life meaningful. Positive thinking leads to conservation of one's energy, whereas the negative thinking leads to quick dissipation of his or her energy. Brain consumes major share of one's energy. Anger, hatred, jealousy, being envious, all these things enervate the beings, whereas joy, smile, love, compassion, mercy, all rejuvenate the beings. Positive thinking utilises the mind and the brain, positively and quite effectively; therefore, performance of a being improves significantly with positive thinking. A being, who always speaks truth, operates his or her life from the fifth energy centre or chakra known as the Vishuddha Chakra. This energy centre is located at the base of the throat. It is at the centre of the Larynx. The guesses, utterances, slip of tongue statements and predictions made by such beings, become true, and turn out to be reality in the life later or sooner. Try to read the mind of others. Make effective communication with others by maintaining constant eye-to-eye contacts with them. It creates hypnotic effects, and then the subject or the object obeys all the orders as given. It is a secret of effective instructions-following by the subordinates. Spread love, affection and joy. Try to win the hearts of others. Winning the hearts, is winning their life. Exercise empathy, sympathy and the inclusivity. Be honest, real, genuine, truthful and hilarious, without vanity and affectations. Vishuddha is a Sanksrit language word, which means purifying the body from various harmful substances. This throat chakra i.e. Vishuddha Chakra, restores the energy by detoxifying all impurities of body and mind. One's performance is essentially his or her mind's performance. Manage the mind in order to manage the performance in life. Think good and act good, as it is the only mantra of good performance in one's life.

CHAPTER THIRTY

The God

The God is the energy of the creation. God is the ultimate consciousness. God is omnipotent, omniscient, and omnipresent. The God is everywhere, and yet, nowhere. The God has every shape and size, and yet, no shape and size. God is an experience, rest all about the God, is being's imagination about the God. Though faith and belief are very powerful and also work, yet there is a chance that faith is not the fact. The God is energy landscape, which is spread all over in this entire creation. This energy landscape touches every point of the space, therefore, there is some or other form of creation, or life, or some other effect, at every point of the space. Space is a natural creation, and it is for real, but the time is mind's creation, an illusion, and the notion of time is purely unreal. The concept of time, created by the mind, helps the brain and the memory in the analyses of situations and effects, and then storing some or all of these. There is nothing like time in reality. Time is an assumption. Past, present and future are the same point, and not the distinct points of time axis. The energy of this creation is the God. Energy creates power(s). This creation is run, managed and administered through and by a certain hierarchical system, where energy is at its top, powers in the middle and the effects at the bottom. The supreme, the energy of the creation, i.e. the God, has delegated its powers down the line to the gods. Creation, sustenance and destruction are the powers. Fire, water, air, light, sound etc. are the effects. These effects then create situations and circumstances in the life of the beings, where they need to think and act in sagacious manner. Power (to the gods) is the delegation of authority by the supreme energy (the God) for the purpose of effective and efficient administration of this entire creation, which primarily includes the life on the earth and other realms and dimensions, based on certain principles. These principles are executed through the laws like Law of Equity, Law of Attraction, Law of Karma etc. These powers further create the effects like effects of gravitation, electricity and magnetism, light and sound etc.. There is only one God (supreme energy), and then many gods (powers). This creation is a play, created by the energy, its powers, and their effects. These gods work under the clearly delegated authority of the God. The God is highest state, the highest form of purity of thoughts and the actions. No being can ever become the God. When a soul attains a certain level of purity, the supreme energy (the God) merges that soul, which is also energy, into itself. Thus, that soul gets rid from the trap of birth and death and then rebirth, and thus, attains the state of salvation, liberation, peace and ultimate happiness, known as the Nirvana. Physical plane i.e. earth, is a punishment ground full of tests. Every being taking birth here, has to undergo the pains, trials and tribulations and the miseries, which he or she has earned by him or herself, through his or her thoughts and actions i.e. deeds. The sole purpose of life on the earth is going through all these pains, in order to experience the life, and then correct the self, so that self's soul evolution and advancement takes place. Once the soul achieves a certain level of its advancement, it is being freed from the shackles of birth and death, and also, the associated pains on the earth. Life on earth is a test life. A real test is never simple, but hard. If a test is simple, then it is not a test, but a mild experience. God loves its every soul. Soul is an element of the God. Mind tests the soul at every moment of its journey on the physical plane, i.e. the earth. Mind should not work against the soul, but for the soul. Therefore, mind management is quite necessary. One's mind should not work against him or her. Positive and negative powers have been deliberately created by the supreme energy (the God), in order to create all kinds of situation and effects like good or bad, true and false, beautiful and ugly, truth and lie, mercy and cruelty etc., for the purpose of soul's testing. Interestingly, soul is trapped by the negative powers, due to infatuation by its false and sinister alluring beauty, charm, power, attraction and comfort. The path of truth and goodness is rough, long and painful, and the journey is very arduous. The path created by the negative powers in the life is quite smooth, short, pleasurable and simple. If there is an easy gain in the life, be careful, as it may be a trap or bait thrown by the negative powers. Hard work, and the life led on principles, eliminates the chances of interference by the negative powers in one's life. Life is a continuous journey. Life is a continuum. Life is infinite. There is a certain afterlife, i.e. the life after the death. Soul never dies. Soul is the true identity of a being. At death, only the physical body is shed, and the soul leaves the body, and waits for a new body to re-enter. The journey of soul after physical death of being depends upon his or her karmic accumulations of the present and the past journey of life.

Soul has no gender. Gender is its manifestation type; the type or kind of soul (energy) association with a body (matter) at the time of birth on the physical plane, and the basis is a certain kind of experiencing. This creation has many realms or planes or dimensions. Earth is a physical plane, and a lower plane, with lower vibrational level, whereas, higher planes are non-physical, and these non-physical planes are spiritual in nature with higher vibrational levels. Always surround yourself with other beings, which appreciate and motivate you, believe in you, empower, support and uplift you. Thought is a power. Thinking is powerful. It is the positive thinking only, which helps in the process of soul's evolution and advancement, and ultimately attaining the God, which is the only purpose of life. As a lost child frantically searches for his parent(s) in a crowded fair or at a bustling place, similarly, the beings on the earth are the individuated souls and are lost in this madding world, but their all thoughts and actions must be in the direction of finding their true parent (the God). Parents on earth are physical plane are temporary, and last only for the duration of one journey of life on the earth, but the God is the spiritual parent of all souls, and is permanent, and always accompanies the soul, till it is not merged back into it (the God), and becomes one with it for good. Positive thinking is the only pathway to reach the God.

CHAPTER THIRTY-ONE

Prayer And Positive Thinking - Power Of Prayer

Raise positive energy, and also, the positive vibrations by doing prayers, and chanting. Light and sound have serious impacts on the quality of one's life, and various related life phenomena. Use lights and sounds in proper ways for better impacts in the life, therefore, creating correct and meaningful outcomes in the life. Prayer is the words, which one uses, while speaking to the God or god(s). Prayer is the only weapon to win the unseen battles of the life. Prayer brings blessings in one's life. The God hears, heeds to, and answers, all true prayers. The God delivers what is best, through one's prayers. Trust the timings of action of the God. Pray to the God for well-being of the self, and the others. A true prayer is always wrapped with the faith, and given with the hope, and then, communicated with love and care. Prayer further strengthens the willpower. It is the willpower, which has the ability to defeat all other powers. Do meditation. Meditation and Sudarshan Kriya help clean one's bad karma. Karma is the basis of everything in the life and the whole creation. Karma creates impressions in the energy, i.e. the energy landscape, which spreads all over in this entire creation. This energy is one's individual consciousness, the universal consciousness and the God. One's thoughts become his or her spoken words, and then, the spoken words become his or her actions, and finally, actions become his or her personality. The journey of life is never short for any being. The God is never discriminatory in its plans and actions. It is the being only, which understands the life and its purpose quite late in his or her journey of life, and by the time he or she understands the life and its very purpose, it is already too late, and now, it is the time for him or her to return to the God. Prayer aligns the beings with the divinity. Prayer changes the beings, which in turn, changes their lives. Prayer and meditation both, influence the state of mind. Mind affects the body. Thus, prayers help, control and eliminate, the anxiety, moroseness, blood pressure, sleep, digestion and the breathing. Prayers influence one's thinking, and make it positive. Prayer energises the hearts of beings through the powers of the spirit(s). Prayer is the process of reaching up to the God. Prayer is the journey from physical to non-physical. Every prayer is listened to, and also, answered. Have faith and belief. Have patience. There is a definite God's plan for every being, and the life moves according to that only. Prayer is a conversation with the God. Prayer develops a relationship at the personal level, with the God. God does not give what one desires, but gives, what one best deserves. Be thankful, obliged and beholden to the God, and get contented with what is there in the life. One always gets more than what he or she deserves. The God is full of compassion. No being is rich here on earth, but all are poor only. Reach richness lies in one's thoughts, words and the action, and good thoughts, words and action, is the only path to reach the God.

CHAPTER THIRTY-TWO

The Nature

The creator and the creation are not different and separate, but one and the same, and also, well integrated into one another. Nature is the best teacher of life. Nature teaches attention and concentration. Nature is always positive, in all its aspects and acts. There is a stronger cause for every effect. Nature is the phenomena of the physical world considered collectively. Nature includes landscapes, features and products of earth, plants, animals, water, weather etc.. Nature works on positive thinking. Nature is all powerful. Power of nature is the power of positivity. Nature has answer to every question of the life. Look deep and deeper into the nature, so as to understand the creation and the creator. Nature contains beauty and knowledge. Nature is a healer. Nature gives peace of mind. Nature is a valuable treasure, therefore, preserve it, and save it. Nature's wilderness demonstrates the spirit of freedom, which is the characteristic of the soul. Nature teaches patience, and demonstrates the power of patience. Nature also demonstrates the powers of faith and belief. What one believes, one gets. Just wait for it to come in the life with unshakeable belief, deep-rooted faith and profound patience. Nature is the art drawn by the almighty. Nature is serene and silent. Silence is very powerful. Talk to the nature, appreciate its ethereal beauty and charm, and it will make experience various dimensions, and help in finding the true self or the real self. Nature is musical. Nature creates the effects of colours, smell, light and sound. Nature, like a responsible parent and a responsible teacher, corrects and compensates for, bad effects and outcomes, which get created due to the bad actions of beings. Nature through its events, demonstrates all the powers of the God. Nature exhibits love, sympathy, caring, sharing, consideration and correction. Nature teaches good parenting and friendship. Nature is always correct. Nature is perfect. Nature is the God. Existence of nature is necessary for the survival of beings. Nature is the source of life. Beings, which live close to the nature, are more healthy, happy and creative. Nature reduces anxieties, stresses, worries and tensions. Nature is very powerful anti-depressant. Life begins in the nature, and also, ends in the nature. Nature works at all the levels, viz. the levels of spirit, mind and the body. Nature helps restore one's mental, spiritual and the physical health to their best states. Nature benefits all beings without discrimination in all its domains, viz. spiritual, cognitive, social, physiological and psychological. Play sports, open in the nature. Nature always inspires and motivates others. Plant more and more trees to enrich the nature. Trees improve the quality of the air. Air is the force of life. Respect the nature. Spend maximum time with the nature. Walk on the grass and feel its healing touch. Nature changes everything in the life quite effectively with its subtle influences and impacts.

CHAPTER THIRTY-THREE

You Can Create The Kind Of World You Wish For

As is the food, so is the mind, and so will be the body. Thought is the food for the mind. World is a set of experiences of a being. Every being has different experiences of life, so he or she has different world. If thinking of a being is positive, then his or her world will also be positive. But if, his or her thinking is negative, then his or her world will also be negative. Thoughts, words and actions make the quality of life, and directly affect the life. Experiences are created by the mind. Thus, one's world is his or her mind's creation. Mind, if managed properly, will create the kind of the world, one wish for. Work on the mind. Mind is managed by mediation, yoga, doing lots of physical work, playing sports, working on passion areas and hobby, doing prayers, being in the company of good and positive beings, and creating good and positive thoughts. Empower self through integration with the nature. Nature will empower you then. The secret doors of the universe will get open then. Work on the self. Identify the real self. Be honest. Connect with the God. God is inside every being. Search the divinity inside. One's world is actually inside. All life experiences are essentially inside out. All outer experiences are experiences arising within the body, which are actually created by the mind inside. These experiences are the experiences of the spirit and soul, and created by the mind. Get enlightened. Read good motivational books. Read religious and spiritual books. It is the power of faith, which makes everything possible in the life. The power of hope makes everything to work, and the power of love makes everything beautiful in the life. Each day of the life, and also, each moment of the life, must be an outcome of the effective use of these three powers. Worrying does not take away tomorrow's troubles, but simply takes away today's peace. One can live happily, if he or she resolves to live happily, otherwise he or she cannot. Understand the life. Understand the game of life. Life is a game. Play it well. Involve in adventures for gaining experiences, knowledge and wisdom. Explore and experience the God. Do mystical experiments. Connect with the visible and invisible power of the creation. Take help of spirits. Invoke and entreat your spirit guide for guidance. Listen to the gut or the hunch. Be obliged and thankful to the entire creation and its creator. The one, who gives birth, also gives the death. If birth is joyful, then death should also be joyful. Every event has some greater purpose. Events are the part of the life's design. Respect the decisions and the actions of the nature and the God. A being once born never dies. Real birth is the birth of the spirit or soul in the higher dimension, and not the birth of the body. On the physical plane i.e. earth, it is just a transformation of energy in the form of birth and death. Soul is energy. Transformation is the very characteristic of this creation. Change is the only constant in this creation.

Matter changes over the time. But the energy does not, and remains constant. Energy manifests itself differently each time through its suitable association with the matter. We are our own gods. We are our own creators. We write our own destiny, since we create our own karma. Thought and words are also karma. Every thought creates karma, either good or bad, depending upon the quality of the thought. Karma is the basis of this whole creation, species forms, life forms, relationships, duration of journey of life of beings, the afterlife, life between lives (LBL), and the life beyond. Life is eternal with no end. We come here, and enact different roles every time in this world drama. Mukti or liberation or salvation or Moksha gives a good riddance from the cycle of birth and death, which is a big trap. Create karma thoughtfully by conscious living. Use the powers of subconscious mind. Learn the art of living, and also, the art of dying. There is a whole world inside of every being. And, what is inside us, is definitely our own creation, and cannot be others. It is the power of positive thinking only, which creates a joyful, beautiful and positive world.

CHAPTER THIRTY-FOUR

Work On Hobbies And Stay Positive

Hobby is something that one does very regularly for self-pleasure. Hobbies are distractions from worries and troubles of the life. Hobby brings joy and happiness, and enriches the life of a being. Hobby gives fun, and also, provides an opportunity to learn newer skills at the same time, and thus, makes the being more and more creative. One's hobby is one's positive engagement. Hobby is an act based on positive thinking. Hobbies make one's heartbeats to match with the beats of the creation. It is the state of resonance of the frequencies and vibrations of the creation and the creator. Hobbies help in one's integration with the nature, and experiencing the goodness of the existence, and the God. A work done with passion eventually becomes one's hobby. Hobbies beat the age, and keep the doldrums away. Some productive hobbies for happy life are, painting, sculpting, clay or wax modelling, writing, reading, collecting, growing, gardening, listening to the music, cooking, doing stand-up comedy, upcycling the trash and turning it into new products, rehashing, building electronics, model making, stretching the body, practising art and craft, photography, playing musical instruments, grooving on with dancing, rock climbing, mountaineering, bungee jumping, walking, moving the body. Most successful people in the world are avid and voracious readers. Hobbies are the best ways for developing the positive attitude, and also, achieving the success and happiness in the life. Practising hobby develops one's powers of concentration and attention. Hobbies make law of attraction to work. Hobby makes the mind peaceful. Hobbies boost confidence and the self-esteem. Hobby shapes one's identity. Spending time on hobbies improves one's mental health, and also, the overall well-being. Beings with hobbies are less likely to suffer from the problems related to the stress, low mood, and depression. Hobbies make one to feel happier and relaxed. Do mediation and yoga. Make these hobbies. Practise various methods of spirituality and empower the self. Empowering the self is advancing the soul, which in turn, results in the start of one's journey on the path of reaching the God.

CHAPTER THIRTY-FIVE

Meditation, Yoga And Sports - Effective Tools For Positive Thinking

Meditation, Yoga and sports defy the age. Age is of the body only which is matter, and not of the soul, which is energy. Soul inside the body is the phenomenon of association of energy with the matter. All souls have same age, and it also same as the age of this whole creation. Karma is the energy created and sent out by the being, whereas destiny is the energy coming towards the being. Always win the fight within own self. But get defeated at times, when there is a fight with the loved ones. It is a mantra for happy, good and long relationships based on positive thinking. There will be fights, opinion difference and rifts in the life. But good relationships and happy life are above all these. Meditation is engaging in contemplation or reflection. Meditation involves mental exercises like concentration on one's breathing, or repetition of a particular mantra. Meditation involves techniques like mindfulness or focusing the mind on a particular object or thought or an activity. Meditation hones up power of attention and concentration, and increases the levels of one's awareness. Meditation helps in achieving a mentally clear and an emotionally calm stable state of mind. Meditation is a journey of reaching a heightened level of spiritual awareness. Meditation nourishes and blossoms the divinity within. Meditation is the process of tuning the self with the inner universe, and also, listening to it, whereas, prayer is the process of talking to the universe. In meditation, mind quietens, and soul starts speaking. Inner silence is actually never silent, but gives answers to all small and big problems of the life. Meditation is magical in nature, and does miracles. Mediation is quite necessary for self-growth. Self-growth is the desire to become a better version of oneself with every passing moment of journey of life. Meditation dissolves unawareness. Meditation produces a deep state of relaxation. Meditation simply tranquilises the mind. Various meditation techniques, which can be easily followed, are mantra medication, spiritual meditation, progressive relaxation, focussed meditation, transcendental meditation and movement meditation. Be different in order to get different in the life. God's love is more than enough in the life. God catches beings, when beings fall. God wipes beings tears, when beings cry. God holds beings, when beings are sad. And, God puts beings back together, when beings are broken. Yoga is based on an extremely subtle science. Yoga focuses on bringing harmony between the mind and the body. Yoga is an art and science of healthy and perfect living. Yoga is a Sanskrit word, meaning 'to join'. Yoga is for the soul. Yoga quietens the mind. Yoga discovers the sense of oneness with the nature and the divinity. Yoga is looking at self from within. Life is not about what one has lost so far, but it is all about, what one can still grow and develop. Life is similar to a tree, which never bothers about the dropping flowers, but it is always busy making new and newer blossoms. Learn the lessons of life from the nature. Nature is the best teacher. Live with the nature, and according to the nature, then there will be no sorrows in the life, but peace and happiness will prevail. Adventure, explorations, experiencing and innovation, is the life. Sports are physical games or activities, which one does as exercises, or simple does because he or she enjoys doing it. Never say "never", as limits like fears, are never real, but are simply an illusion created by Maya, the illusory cosmic element. Life is a sport, play it well. Live the life like a sportsperson. Do not shirk any difficult situation or challenging circumstance in the life. Dare to face the life as it is, and experience it. The purpose of life is, to experience the life. Life becomes easy by adopting positive thinking. One misses 100% of the shots, which he or he does not take. Never be afraid of failures. There is nothing like success or failure, but two types of experiences in the life. Life in itself is a long, inexplicable, less understood and less explored experience for normal beings, but always an enriching and fulfilling experience for the enlightened ones.

CHAPTER THIRTY-SIX

Use Right Words

Words spoken by a being create his or her karma. Karma is the basis of whole creation and the existence. One's quality of life depends upon his past and present karma. Present karma will create his or her future kind and quality of life. Positive words when spoken create positive karma, whereas, negative words when spoken, create negative karma. Thinking creates thoughts. Even thoughts create karma. Thoughts then create words. Words then create action. Words and actions both, also create karma. Therefore, always use right words in the given journey of life. What we think, we attract in our life. Word is a single distinct meaningful element, either of speech or of the writing. Words once uttered, can only be forgiven, but not forgotten easily. Words are quite powerful. Words have the power of creation and destruction. Words contain the power of creativity. Words are healers. Words have power of spreading love, peace and happiness. One's actions must live up to his or her spoken words. Words of kindness mean a whole new world for a being, which is into his or her tougher times of the journey of life. Words are, innocent yet deliberate, good yet evil, powerless yet potent, and caring and loving yet full of abhorrence. Use the right words to create a right world. Your words are your personality. Words create impact. Words create one's attitude. Words create world(s). Words are balmy and soothing, and allay wrath and hatred. Words are magical, and give unlimited power. Words create problems, and also, the solutions. Power of mantra, is essentially the power of its sounds, which lies within its curated words. Words have the ability to push the limits. Gods always used sweet words. All great souls of past and present, never used / use harsh words, but only sweet words. Selection of words is an art. Mind management helps in proper selection of the right words. Words have the power to organise the self, and also, the others. Be the best version of the self with the use of proper words. Poets and media use the power of words quite effectively in their actions / vocation. Word is manifestation of one's intent. Intent is micro and quite subtle, whereas, thought is macro and perceivable. Intent creates thoughts. Positive thinking creates right words, and in turn, right words affect create more positive thinking. Power of positive thinking is the power of right words and the right behaviour. Words are the impressions of the being(s), and his or her signatures of life. Right words create right life. Right words are the words of goodness and the godliness. Read books of religion, life engineering and the spirituality, which will help one in developing the habit of using the right words in the life, and then getting benefitted by the power of words. Prayer is a collection of right words. Power of prayer is the power of words. Consciously spoken words contain his or her intent and the thought(s). The powers of the universe and the creation are the powers of right words and the positive thoughts arising out of positive thinking. Right words are like right food. Right words create right mental, emotional and physical health.

CHAPTER THIRTY-SEVEN

Right Imagination

What one imagines, he or she creates that. Wish is the first stage of process of imagination. One's surroundings are his or her imagination(s). Whatever is felt repeatedly, is experienced by him or her. One's behaviour is always greater than his or her knowledge. In many life situations and circumstances, knowledge may fail, but a correct and appropriate behaviour is always able to handle it very well. Imagination is the faculty or action of forming newer concepts, ideas and images of the objects, which are otherwise not present to the senses. Imagination is a mental picture. Imaginations are created by the mind. A positive imagination is an outcome of positive thinking. Imaginations are very powerful. Power of imagination is essentially the power of affirmations. Imaginations have the ability to make Law of Attraction to work in the life. Always imagine positive and good, for positive and good results in the life. We create our own lives. We are our own gods. Imagination is important than the knowledge. Knowledge is limited, but imagination is unlimited. Imagination makes evolution to happen. Imagination stimulates progress. Imagination becomes reality. At the beginning, God is an imagination only, but later, the God is experienced. Powers of faith and belief are derived from the power of imagination. "Deep-rooted faith and infallible and unshakeable belief" is the mantra for overall success in the life. A right imagination opens the secrets doors of the universe. All worldly experiences are created out of one's imagination. Worry is a negative imagination, and a sheer waste of powers of imagination. Do not use imagination for creating anxiety. What is sense-perceived as reality was an imagination first. Imagine of good and sweet relationships, all relations will improve, and ultimately become sweet. Imagination leads to creativity. Imagination leads to knowledge creation. Imagination leads to the enlightenment. Imagination is the inconceivable force, having the ability to do magic and miracles. One's imaginations are preview to his or her life situations. Imagination is the workshop of the mind. All sense-perceptions are wrong, if imagination is out of focus. Make use of artificial imagination. Artificial imagination is also known as synthetic imagination or simply machine imagination. Artificial imagination is artificial simulation of human imagination. Start using conscious thinking to its greatest capacity. Synthetic imagination and creative imagination are two forms of imagination. Subsections of imagination are dreams, empathy, strategic imagination, effectuated imagination, emotional imagination, imaginative fantasy, memory reconstruction and intellectual or constructive imagination. Imagination leads to formation of vivid mental images and phonological passages. Imagination also creates analogies and narratives. Imagination is manifestation of memory. Tantra empowers the imagination(s), and makes the mental processes to act like physical processes, and thus, creating imagined manifestations in the life as reality. Use power of imagination for self-elevation. Purify the mind by chanting the name of the God and using the power of visualisation. Images are always more powerful than the words. Power of thoughts is used by imagination(s) in order to make the mind to work on the matter i.e. what is physical. Imaginations use the power of subconscious mind. Therefore imagine, but always right.

CHAPTER THIRTY-EIGHT

Stop Negative Self-Talk

Negative self-talk is too disturbing, and quite detrimental. The mind talks to itself in self-talk. Self-talk is internal dialogue. Every thought is a creation of being. Thought is energy. Source of thought is information. What is ingested, taken inside, and assimilated, affect the quality of thoughts. One's senses bring the outer things, inside the being. What is seen, smelt, heard, tasted and felt, is created as information by the brain. Brain only does, what the mind says to it. Mind is the master, and brain is its slave. Train and manage the mind in such a way, that negative information is not generated. Positive self-talk is always good, as it promotes being's mental, emotional and the physical health. Information is the basis or source of all self-talk. Quality of food directly affects the body, and the quality of emotions directly affects the mind. Being in physical form is an outcome of sync among the body, mind and the spirit. What is seen, read or heard, create information, which affects the emotions, and therefore, affects the mind. Mind has its own memory. Information created and going inside the being is stored in his or her subconscious mind. Subconscious mind is too powerful. Use subconscious mind's powers carefully and consciously. Stop mind from meandering. One's life is an outcome of what is absorbed by the body, and contained by the mind inside it. Work on the quality of information, and thus, negative self-talk will be eliminated. Do emotional detox from time to time by following various methods and techniques, as stated in the spirituality. Meditation, Yoga and physical exercises are best methods for stopping any negative self-talk. Work on thoughts and their quality. Start the day, with the name of the God in the morning, with high energy. Overuse of gadgets like phone, TV, computer etc., are the sources of poor quality and miserable life. Happiness is a habit, practise it. Do everything with a good heart. Do not expect anything from anybody in life. It is the mantra to stop any possible disappointment, and thus, living happily. Trees lose all their leaves at least once a year, but still, they stand tall and straight, and wait for better days to come with new sprouts. Bide the time. Learn from the nature. Nature is the best teacher. Live in nature's style. Nothing is yours, yet all is yours. Always live in magnanimity. Intention is very important among all things, aspects and factors of the life, which must be pure and good always. A being with good intent and thoughts is angel sort, and a being with bad intent and thoughts is devil sort.

CHAPTER THIRTY-NINE

Positive Thinking And Age

Age is just a number. Do not make age, a feeling. Win over the vices. Live a meaningful and fulfilling life. Life in itself is a thrilling and a great learning experience, and nothing more than that. We neither win in the game of the life nor lose. Life is a lesson, an experience. Events of the life are the lessons of the life. All in this creation is an illusion, simply a creation of the mind. Change the state of the mind, thing(s) will change in the life. Keep the soul pure. Satisfaction lies in the efforts, and not in the attainments. Full efforts itself is a full victory. Winning without risk is like triumph without glory. Always have a desire to succeed, but if you do not get success, do not repent and stop, but keep making efforts. Life is like a bicycle ride, if you stop, you fall, therefore, keep moving. Have urge to reach your full potential. This desire and urge will unlock door(s) to personal experience(s). Be a performer in the journey of the life. Many stumbles in the life, prevent many fall. Therefore, stumbles are necessary in the life. Each stumble is an important lesson of the life. Opportunities are never lost in the journey of life. These are taken by the beings, which are willing, and also, ready to catch. Our age is infinite. We all had always existed here, and also, will exist here forever. We are energies. This matter association (physical or gross body) is ephemeral. Energy manifests itself through matter association and for this reason only, birth happens. Death is for rebirth, a new and another experience of the life. Life is a continuum. Our real self or true identity is the spirit inside and not the body. We are energies (soul or spirit) and not the matter (physical or gross body). Age is not a barrier for anything in the life. Do not let it become a limitation of the mind. Do not mind the age, and the age will not matter. The life is all about mind management. Age always adds to the wisdom, understanding, the inner beauty, and the styles of the beings. Count the age and the life by the number of true friends and the smiles, and not by the years passed or the tears shed. Age is a natural way of enlightenment. Age automatically brings in positive thinking. Age teaches what the life is. Age reveals that there are no precise answers in the life to its problems, but there are only stories. Grow up and do not grow old. Age is a record of one's life. Positive thinking has all positive effects on the age, and also, on all the factors related to ageing process. Age is a state of mind. This age is just a chronological number. Eat better and less, have good quality enough and proper sleep, eliminate stresses worries and anxieties, do lots of physical exercises regularly and do not lead a sedentary lifestyle. Doing so, significantly slows the ageing process. Help others. Connect with the nature. Follow passions and hobbies. Decide at the level of the mind, not to grow old, and you will not become old. Quality of thoughts and the way of thinking, matters to the real ageing process. Stay patient, and trust your journey of life. Have faith and belief in the God and his acts. Positive thinking keeps a being young and healthy.

CHAPTER FORTY

Positive Thinking And Success

Success is the fact that one has achieved what he or she wants. Success is the creation of mind. In the physical world, success has been ill-defined and wrongly understood by the beings. The real parameter of success is advancement of the soul, peace in the life, and experiencing the God. In the game of life, there is nothing like success, or failure. It is success only every time. There is nothing like “an end”, of anything, in the game of life, but, in the life, there is always a beginning of same thing which has just ended, either in the same form, or other form. Start each day of the life with a smile. Do prayer to bless the ways. Stay cheerful. Make life beautiful and peaceful. Life is easy. One can make the life easy by ignoring bad things, and accepting good things. The real art of knowing in the life is, knowing what to ignore in the life. Majority of decisions in the journey of life are not ours, but are taken by the nature for us, and remaining decisions are governed by the factor of time. Destroy the evils by using the powers of prayer. Invoke the divinity. Pray to God to get the powers to, withdraw, cooperate, let go, face, tolerate, decide, accept and discern. Do not consume the mind with negativity.

Think positive. Challenges come in the life. It is the design of life, and it is for every being. Success is because of challenges. If there is no challenge in the life, there will be no success in the life either. Success or failure both, are the outcomes of one's thoughts. Success is first created in the mind, before it turns into the reality. In this physical world, i.e. earth, try to create a big and bigger family. Whole creation should be the part of one's family. Every other thing is just another you, and not separated and distinct from you. Try making the family beyond the blood. Never do discrimination. God did not create its creation to live in discrimination, jealousy and hatred, but in a complete cohesion, love and peace. Life is too simple to lead with simple and positive thoughts, and becomes, too difficult to lead when thoughts get complex and become negative. Every being has its own definition of success. However, a single definition of success in the journey of life is "contentment, fulfilment and happiness in the life". Actions create results. Positive actions create positive results and the success. Have patience, and use the powers of faith and belief. Only those beings win, which carry the winning attitude. A right attitude is only created by the right and positive thinking. The things beyond control are acts of the God. Nothing in the life is painful. Pain is created in the mind. Pleasure is also created in the mind. Train the mind to derive pleasure from all acts, events and circumstances of the journey of life. Death is not bad. Sleep gives maximum comfort. Each sleep is going into the lap of death each time. But with each awake, death returns you, to continue the remaining journey of the life. In death, death simply accepts you, with no further return for this journey of life, but prepares you for a next much better life. It is the world drama. Death gives maximum comfort to the soul. All processes of nature are for betterment. No act of the God is bad, but simply a blessing in the life, no matter what. Every failure in the life, takes one, close and closer to the success. Life of each being is pre-scripted. So do not complain, but accept whatever comes the way, in the journey of the life, and keep moving on. It is positive thinking and success. Success is an experience, out of many experiences of the journey of life. Success lies in one's thoughts and experiences. In essence, life is an experience, which must be fulfilling and gratifying.

CHAPTER FORTY-ONE

Positive Thinking And Richness

Thinking matters. Mind has great capacity. Thoughts are created in the mind first, and then, processed by the brain, in order to convert them into the reality in the life. Think of richness, in order to become rich. Affirmations and positive thinking, both work. Work on the mind. Affirm of richness in stillness, think of become rich. Do meditation. Affirm self with good thoughts and words. What is thought materialises. Change the mental dialogues suitably. All power is within the being. We are gods. Awaken the sleeping soul. Meditation and Yoga manage the mind. Do these. One's mind-health should be perfect. Mind management is the biggest life skill. Many problems, which cannot be solved, should be left to the God, and to the factor of time. Believe that its solution will be good, no matter what, and when. Have patience in life. Believe in the powers of faith and belief. Peace of mind and a happy life, is the real richness in life. Experiencing the God in the life is real richness. Eliminate pride, ego, greed, hatred, anger, selfishness, lust, negativity, delusion and jealousy from life, by positive thinking. A being devoid of all these negative characteristics is the real rich. Always speak politely, in order to seek a polite answer. One who has love in his or her heart, is admired by all everywhere every time. Richness lies in one's mind, heart and the soul. Richness lies in one's words and actions. Real richness of life is not physical gains, money, power, wealth, assets and success. Real richness is spiritual in nature, and not physical in nature. We are spirits, and not the physical body. Do things which go with the spirit. This physical body has to be shed here, one day. All physical things will be left on the physical plane. Peace, satisfaction, contentment, fulfilling life experiences, happiness, sweet relationships with others are the indicators of real richness in the life. Think positive and act positive. Be kind to others. Be in love with the nature. Nature is the biggest mother. Loving the nature is, loving the God. Keep body, mind and spirit in sync always. Talk to the spirits. Invoke the powers of the universe. Prayers are very powerful, and are always listened to. Ask for richness in words, actions and behaviour. Understand the life. We all had been here in the physical domain innumerable times before, but did the same mistakes every time. Real richness takes one out of the trap of birth-death and then rebirth. Move towards from being ordinary to extraordinary i.e. greatness. Greatness has to do nothing with the physical riches. Greatness lies in one's nobility of character. Be magnanimous. Learn from the acts of great souls, which visited the planet earth i.e. the physical plane from time to time. God had sent them. Emulate them. Life is too short to enjoy, and too long to suffer. Enjoyment and sufferings are the two out of many other creations of the mind. Mind is subtle body, and body is gross mind. All creations of the mind are fictitious, and not real. These two i.e. enjoyment and sufferings, emerge from one's thoughts, words and actions. Enjoyment and suffering are the effects, and not the cause. Richness is the effect caused by positive thinking.

CHAPTER FORTY-TWO

Confidence And Depression

Gift a good life to self. Never let confidence go below a certain level, as it may lead to depression. Belief and confidence are necessary ingredients of a successful life. Confidence is, aplomb or self-possession or assurance. Confidence is a state of mind, which is marked by easy coolness and sheer freedom. Confidence is freedom from uncertainty. Confidence is freedom from diffidence or embarrassment. Confidence stresses faith in oneself, and also, in one's powers, that too, without suggestion of any arrogance or a conceit. Overconfidence is excessive confidence. Both, overconfidence and underconfidence are unwanted cognitive biases. Bias is a strong feeling, and often, not based on fair judgement or facts. Underconfidence is characterised by an underestimation of self-ability(s) to perform task(s) successfully. Underconfidence is underrating of self-performance relative to that of others. Depression is a feeling of unhappiness, which usually lasts for a long time. Depression is a medical condition. Depression has physical signs like inability to sleep. Confidence and fortitude determine one's success in his or her life. Confidence is power. Confidence is self-approval. Being confident, in itself, is winning, before actually winning or getting success. Depression is self-imprisonment. Do not get angry, and express anger. Never become indignant. There are other decent positive behavioural ways and other manifestations for display of such emotions. Always converse. Talking is views and opinion sharing. Talks about the issues and problems must be frequent, without any emotional accumulation, and then, leading to its undesired and inapt outburst at some moment. Do not be fragile in the life. Anger leads to depression. Anger is a slow poison. Anger saps the soul of its power. Words used and the language spoken must be proper, always. Anger is losing control on the self. Never lose control on the self. Finish all your fears and anxieties by working on these. Positive thinking eliminates anger and depression. Always, think good and positive. Do not get addicted to bad behavioural traits. Vibrations of beings must be positive, always. Every being must be emotionally strong and healthy. Depression is an illness, which greatly impairs one's emotional health. Creativity, awareness, happiness, health etc., all improve and increase, when there is no anger, and no depression. Confidence and depressions are outcomes of good and bad mind management, respectively. Give value to the self. Empower the self. Remain stable in the life, and always respond with stability and responsibility. Every being is a powerful soul. Heal the spirit. Do Dhyana, meditation, yoga, physical exercises, connect with the nature, and drink and eat, good and well. We are our own creators. We are gods. We create our own reactions and responses, and no one else. Never react, but always respond sensibly at every moment, and in every situation, of the life. Do not live like a victim. Do not get affected by other's behaviour. One's emotional, mental and physical health is fully in its own right. Heal the self. No one else can ever make one angry, or feel insulted, without his or her permission. Always radiate good energy. One creates his or her own thoughts and feelings. Both, confidence and depression are feelings. Never get irritated and annoyed, as these simply put one, in acute and excruciating pain, with absolutely no meaningful outcomes. Remain happy, and learn to live alone. One is alone, and also, never alone. It is just a perspective about the life. It is simply an understanding of the life. Do meditation in morning, as it is an exercise for the mind. Do meditation in and out of the home, when the life is most busy with every other thing. Mind management is needed most, when the life is too busy, and there are many challenges, and many ups and downs are already happening. Do Raja Yoga. Raja Yoga refers to both, viz. the goal of yoga, and also, the method of attaining it. Take spiritual diet (good food, good thoughts, good actions and good practises) in life for a better emotional health and a better mind management (mental health), and it will eliminate depression and its toll on the health, while always keeping the one confident in his or her life. There is a whole universe within all of us. All our outer world experiences are inner experiences only. Change the way you think. For success, three essential things, which are needed in the life are, practise, dedication and meditation. Practise positive thinking. It is very powerful. It will make you confident, and eliminate the depression. Dedicate the life for every cause of goodness. Goodness is godliness. The journey of life is the journey from manliness to the godliness.

CHAPTER FORTY-THREE

Surviving The Worst Situations Of The Life

Worst situations of the life are, chronic and fatal diseases, deaths, severed relations, repeated failures, accidents, tragedies etc.. Life situations, as good or bad, have been defined by the beings, and not by the nature or the God. What we see, we become. For the majority of beings, their life upbringing and conditioning are wrong. Definitions are created in the minds of the beings. Mind tests the beings, based on their reactions and responses in various perilous and precarious situations of their life, and majority of beings flunk in this test of the mind. Life is a test. Understand the life. Look at the life journey of great souls, son of God, messengers of God, Gurus, and incarnations of the God. Their life journey was never simple, but too arduous. A normal being can never live their kind of life. Always live in ardour. Life is never too simple, for any being. It is we, who make it simple with correct and proper understanding, and mind management, or simply let it remain tough, with no work in that direction. Look at the nature, its events, and a continuously ongoing struggle in the nature. It is the life. Learn from it. Nature is the best teacher of life. This all is a world drama. Do not be serious about anything here. Everything is short-lived. There is a change, happening at every moment in this vast creation. Creation or construction, destruction and reconstruction are the part of this continuous change. It is a continuum. Similarly, birth, death and rebirth are the part of this continuous change of the creation. Nothing, and no being, is permanent here. Kings came, and now, ruins are only there. Good are only remembered. Therefore, become good in life. Matter gets destroyed, only energy prevails, at the last. Matter is never good or bad. It is the energy, which is good or bad. Therefore, energy should be good always. Good energy is the God. Surviving worst situations or winning is not a result, but an action and an attitude towards the life, a habit. Make winning a habit. Work on attitude. Mind creates the attitude. Work on the mind. What love can do, hatred can never do. Freedom is the characteristic of the soul. Fill the hearts will love. In this creation, nothing is yours. Remember, I am another you. When source of everything is same, then how, we can be different. Maya, the illusory cosmic element of the universe has created this false distinction, in order to test us. A folded hand has the power of winning the millions of hearts. Win this world by virtues, and not by the vices. No situation of the life is tough; it is we, who perceive it to be tough. Change the perception, the nature of situation will change. Death is blissful, as we return to our true home. In the journey of life, where we get hands of the God, after death we get the lap of God. Death is peaceful. There is nothing more precious than the peace. There is never an early or a bad death, but it always occurs right, at the right time, at the right space, and in the right situation, as per the best design of life. We all meet again in the Spirit World, which is a non-physical dimension in this vast creation. All those beings, which are presently not in their physical forms, are in their spirit forms. Connect with them at the spirit level, if wished for. In this world drama, there is union, separation and reunion. Spirit has indomitable power of winning at the last, and the resilience, whatever the situation is, in this show and the game of the life. Referee is the God. World witnessed deadly Corona pandemic, it was a tough test of entire humanity, many have died, but a vast majority has survived too. Never give up. Fight tougher situations or circumstances by understanding the situations or the circumstances in their right perspective. Positive thinking provides the necessary endurance, and the needed winning abilities. Do mind management. Life is nothing, but all about the mind management. Do Dhyana, prayers, Meditation and Yoga. Play physical sports. Take good food. Drink lots of water. There is always a helping hand of the God with all us throughout the journey of life. Many spirits, and the Spirit Guide, assist us continuously during the journey of life on earth (physical dimension). Connect with them, and no problem will remain a problem then in the life, but simply becomes an experience of the life. Life is the gift of the God. How a gift can be bad? Dedicate everything, whether good or bad to the God with no hypocrisy. Be clear from the heart. Never have bad feelings. As beings, there is no need to worry for the outcomes, as outcomes or the results are always created by the God, and not by the beings. Just focus on sincere efforts. There is nothing like good or bad, success or failure, joy or sorrow, pleasure or miseries, but these are simply the states of the mind, and essentially a creation of the mind. Have patience. Have faith in self, and belief on the God. It takes every being out of the tougher and worst situations of the life in a magical and mysterious ways. Do not try to understand the magic and mysteries of the universe. Just witness these with neutral minds. When no one is there, always remember, God is there. Look at the heavens, ask for help, and the help comes immediately. We are the children of the God. Parents never leave or abandon their children, not at least in the times of utter despair and gloom. Deserve to be the best child. A right and positive thinking is the only key to survive the worst situations of the life.

CHAPTER FORTY-FOUR

We All Are Alone

We all come to the physical plane, at a different time, and / or in a different space, in each birth. We come alone. We all are alone. We go alone. Individual means, which is not further divisible. Therefore, try to be complete in the self, i.e. the true self or the real self or the ideal self, and become worthy of being called as an individual. True self or real self or ideal self are terms, which describe one's personality domains. These terms mean, who we actually are. It is all about how, one thinks, feels, looks, and acts. One's real self is seen and perceived by the others. True self or real self or ideal self is one's self-image. Only being, him or herself, is solely responsible for results of his or her karma, done in the past and the present. Karma creates consequences, events, situations, circumstances, which cannot be changed, or transferred to other being(s). We all are energies. And, according to individual's energy map or energy landscape, his or her journey of life is being designed. This energy map or energy landscape is created by the individual only, based on his or her thoughts, decisions and the actions. Therefore, being's every thought and action must be consciously and judiciously created / performed. Mind creates confusions. Work on the mind, and bring clarity to it. Energy should be pure. Aura must be clean and bright. Think positive. No relationship in the physical world is for real. Only spirit or soul connections are for real. True love never dies. Only true unconditional love survives all times and spaces, realms and domains, and dimensions, and remains unaffected. True love is sacrificial in nature, and there is no take, but only give. Do not carry expectations from others in life, for a happy life. Every being is unique, and equally loved by the God. The design of the life and the journey of the life for every being are unique, which depends on his or her karma and energy imprints. In this physical world, nothing succeeds like success. Achieve state of Pragya in the life. Pragya or Prajña is the state of full wisdom. Pragya or Prajña refers to the highest and purest form of wisdom, intelligence and understanding. Pragya or Prajña is higher than the knowledge, obtainable by reasoning and inference. It is better to walk alone in the journey of the life for self-spiritual growth. Learn to be by yourself. Beings are not compulsive actions. Our all actions must be purposeful. Evolution of soul is the sole purpose of life. Love yourself. Release all your pains and hurts. Difficulties in the life do not come to destroy, but to help, and finding the real hidden potential. Organise the mind, and all things wished for, will then keep happening in the life. Raise the energies within by using the powers of positive thinking and the subconscious mind. Life is beautiful. Grow consciously, and for that purpose, it is essential to be alone.

CHAPTER FORTY-FIVE

Positive Thinking And Nirvana

Nirvana is the state of peace and happiness in the life, which is achieved after giving up all personal desires. In life, boil ego, and evaporate all worries. Dilute all sorrows and filter every mistake. Then only, life will give the taste of happiness. Nirvana means enlightenment. When sense of individuality disappears, and the sense of universality, individual dissolution and complete integration with the nature appears, Nirvana is achieved. Nirvana is experiencing the heaven. "Vana" means discomforts of life and death. "Nir" means passing beyond. Thus, Nirvana means, simply passing beyond all discomforts of life and death. The eightfold path leading to Nirvana consists of eight simple practices. These eight practices are, right view, right speech, right resolve, right conduct, right effort, right livelihood, right mindfulness, and lastly, the right samadhi. The right Samadhi means meditative absorption or the union. Positive thinking is the basis of this eightfold path leading to the enlightenment or the Nirvana. Real pleasure of life is in "giving", and not in "taking", or hoarding and amassing and showing greed. Greed is excessive need, or a feeling of need beyond the real need. Nirvana makes one to get awake to the realities of the life. Clarity about everything in the life is enlightenment. Memory is not the intelligence. Karma concept emerges from the memory. Freedom from memory is freedom from the self. Various types of memories are genetic memory, atomic memory, evolutionary memory, elemental memory etc., and these all types of memories have their different levels like, articulate and inarticulate, conscious and unconscious etc.. Enlightenment is, not mixing up the two, viz. the memory and the intelligence, but using them separately, may be simultaneously also at times, and very judiciously always, in the journey of life.

CHAPTER FORTY-SIX

Positive Thinking And Salvation

Salvation is, saving a being from the negative powers of evil. This creation has both, viz. goodness and evil, positive and negative energies. Being good and achieving goodness is the very purpose of the life. It is positive thinking, which creates a strong aura of a being, and thus, a being is saved from evils. Bad thoughts entertain and cultivate evils. A positive thinking harbours good thoughts, and such a positive being is only saved by the positive powers and energies of the universe from all prevailing negative powers and negative energies. Salvation rescues somebody or something from danger, disaster etc.. Salvation is, saving from, or delivering from, a sin or harm. Sin is an act, which is against the God's will, and therefore, it is morally wrong. Salvation is achieved through repentance, and faith in the God. Salvation is essential for establishing a very strong bond with the God, while being on the earth in physical form. Salvation is also essential for an eternal life with the God in the heaven after the death. Salvation makes the beings to receive the God's grace continuously. Salvation helps beings to lead a good life here in physical dimension, and after death, in the Spirit World. Only God is the door for salvation. Salvation is essential for soul's evolution and advancement. Salvation makes a being quite powerful. Energy and wisdom both must be used by the beings simultaneously, in their every act of life, as it determines the intensity and profoundness of their life. Energy and wisdom, when used together, make a being very powerful. Become very effective in the life. Positive thoughts conserve one's energies, whereas, negative thoughts dissipate one's energies. Speak less. Reduce movements. Chant mantras, as their reverberations stop the unnecessary wandering and chattering of the mind, and a focussed mind is a very powerful thing. The power of salvation and the power of the mind are essentially the power of the positive thinking.

CHAPTER FORTY-SEVEN

Eliminating All Negative Influences

Whatever thing or situation one repeatedly imagines, he or she creates similar thing or situation in his or her life. Beings must learn, to learn from yesterday, live in today, and dream for beautiful tomorrow. Be the reflection of what you had liked to receive. To receive love, give love. Be truthful, to expect the truth from others. Give respect in order to receive the respect. What we give returns. It is the Law of Karma. In the life, other than the self, nobody else is yours. Always believe and focus on "ABC" of the life. Here, A is ability, B, the behaviour, and C, the character. Protect yourself from the negative energies and the negative influences in the surroundings. Wear Rudraksha. Rudraksha tree grows in Himalayas at high altitudes. Rudraksha is Stonefruit. These dried stones are used as the prayer beads. When ripe, Rudraksha stones are covered by an inedible blue outer fruit. Sometimes, Rudraksha is also called as "Blueberry Beads". Rudraksha has unique vibrations, which can cleanse being's aura. Aura is being's field of light and energy, enveloping him or her. Aura is subtle manifestation of everything of a being. Aura evinces states of mental, emotional and the physical health of a being. These three types of health are always in accordance with one's karmic structure. Rudraksha eliminates the effects of the negative influences in the life of beings. Do not fight the mind. Hold and harbour beautiful positive thoughts. Never react, but always respond. Play divine music. Keep the light of fire. Keep the place clean and everything in good order. These simple things eliminate the effects of negative influences on one's life. Raise the energies within. Purify the body and mind by ingesting proper food and following certain exercises. Do meditation. Drink good amount of clean water. Put strong positive affirmations into the water before drinking. Take water bath, wind bath, mud bath and the fire bath. Use Neem or Nim leaves and sticks for various daily activities. Neem (Azadirachta Indica) is also known as Margosa. Neem is a fast-growing tree of Mahogany family (Meliaceae). Neem is valued as a medicinal plant. Neem is source of organic pesticides. Also, it is used in cosmetics, and in organic farming applications. Mind creates thoughts. Take charge of mind. Thoughts impact the health. Thoughts create feelings. Therefore, purify the mind. Do mind management. Manage the situations and circumstance of the life with positive mind, i.e. positive thoughts. Have positive nature. One's mood is one's choice. In life, everything beyond one's control happens for good. Positive thoughts are very powerful and eliminate all negative influences of life.

CHAPTER FORTY-EIGHT

Excellence

Expect to win, and you will definitely win. Excellence is not a skill, but an attitude. We become, what is repeatedly done. Therefore, excellence should not become just a one-time act, but essentially one's habit. Excellence is all about doing one's best. Excellence is the quality of being very good. Positive thinking brings "excellence" in the life. Impeccable success is the excellence. Quintessence is the excellence. Excellence in behaviour is one's magnanimous character. Excellence is nobility. A positive mind helps achieve excellence in the chosen domain or the walk of life. A positive mind is based on positive thinking. Excellence is not the effect, but a cause. The acts performed must be excellent. Excellence leads to perfection. Excellence in behaviour makes a being liked by all, and very much loved by the nature and the God. Be magnanimous and noble in the character. Love all. Love everything. All will love you. Everything will love you. What we give comes back. Such beings are greatly adored and highly venerated. Full creation is another me, rather me only. Living with this thought, brings true joy, happiness and sheer bliss in the life. All the pains and sorrows of life then vanish in the thin air. We all are created by one creator, then how we can be unrelated. Any other life form is another form of me only. Every being and everything in this cast creation is me, or related to me, or just another me. This thought is the ultimate reality, and it initiates a conversation with every other entity in this universe or the creation. The secret doors of the universe then get open. Being can then use the powers of the universe for his spiritual development. The soul then, is in its good state of purity. The levels of energies within the being rise, and the being becomes vibrant. Soul becomes too powerful then. The purpose of the life is "journey towards perfection through excellence". There is enough for every being in this creation. Never be greedy. Never usurp. Never exploit others. Let every being get his or her share in everything available in the nature. Be good, and demonstrate goodness by actions to others. Happiness in the life is the goal or purpose of life. Happiness is a feeling, which is largely affected by the environment. Therefore, for personal happiness, his or her environment should be good. We affect others, others affect us. Therefore, never ignore any other being or any other thing. Just love all beings and every other thing. It is only the path of excellence, a journey from manliness to godliness. Excellence leads to culmination of advancement of the soul.

CHAPTER FORTY-NINE

Your Work Is Your Worship

Make your work, your worship. Work is meditation. Not only put your mind and body into the work that you do, but put your soul also into that work. Then, that work will become God. Though, one is always doing his or her works, but with such a level of involvement and pleasure in doing the works, he or she is essentially worshipping the God. Work is worship. Great works are always performed with perseverance. Duty is God. Work with joy, then energy comes out from that work, and energises the being and the environment, similar to the prayer. Considering work as worship is a positive thought having immense energy and power. With this thought, "Your work is your worship", no work remains a burden, but turns into a sheer enjoyment and bliss. One's hobbies and passions are the works, which are done as worship. We all have come here in the physical domain to perform some or other work(s). Kind of work depends on one's karma. So never make complain about the kind or type of work. Work is a blessing in life. Our relationships are part of our works. If the work is performed with love, care and consideration, relationships will remain sweet. Taking care of nature and other creatures is part of our work in the journey of life. Prayer, yoga and meditation are other important works of life. One must be affable and sweet-natured. Work when taken as worship, does miracles in the life.

CHAPTER FIFTY

The Right Job

One should be passionate for his or her job, and then only job gets right for him or her. Enthusiasm is the measure of health of a being. One should be enthusiastic to do his or her job. Job must be as per one's hobby, interest and passion. Give your one hundred per cent in the job that you do. What one does, comes back to him or her only. It is only the Law of Karma or Newton's Third Law of Physics. The way to do great works is to love what is being done. Works and the job fill a large part of one's age or journey of life; therefore, try to derive satisfaction and pleasure out of the job being performed, and the works being done. Such a job is only the right job. When thoughts are positive and pure, a being listens to his or her soul, and a right job is then chosen by him or her. A right job is always gratifying. A right job is the job, which one loves, and if, the job is so chosen, and then he or she does not have to work even a single day in his or her life. Job is the book, and the being, which does it, is the author of this book. Opportunities do not come, but are created in the life. Build your own dreams. Fall in love with your job and the works, in order to become successful. One's job is his or her reflection of personality. Earn respect from performed actions. Destiny is consequence of performed actions. Put in better efforts in order to improve the destiny. Destiny can be improved, and also, changed with conscious efforts. Follow the right religion in the life. Religion is an art of life and death. Learn art of death for a happy journey of life on the physical plane, i.e. earth. Making adjustments is the life. Making compromises is the life. Try putting best efforts, such that God himself asks what your wants are, and gives the desired fruits of destiny. Never react, but always respond. Do not let the negative influence penetrate into the life. Raise the level of perception, and identify negative influences, annihilate these, decimate these, before these affect you adversely and negatively. Improve consciousness. Life is a game; learn the tricks of this game of life, in order to play it well, before it gets late. Always think positive and act positive. Positive thinking is very powerful, and only it, can bring in the desired positive results in the journey of life.

CHAPTER FIFTY-ONE

Stop Worrying, Always Stay Happy

Struggles of life shape one to become a better being in his or her journey of life. Life itself is a struggle. Beings come here only to face the struggles of life, and then to learn from each struggle and event. Thoughts create perceptions. Therefore, work on thoughts. Have positive thinking. Positive thinking is very powerful. With positive thinking, no pain, or a problem or a struggle of life remains what it is, but turns into just another experience of the life. Soul has to experience everything during the journey of life. Understand the design of life. Experiencing the life is the purpose of the life. Without experiences in the life, ups and downs in the life, how soul will advance or evolve. There is no reason to worry in the life. Life is a drama. Life is too short and temporary on the physical realm. After death, soul stays in the Spirit World till rebirth on the physical realm. Time and space affect the whole course of one's life. To improve the life, work on the mind. Mind creates everything. It creates every perception. Pleasure and pain are perceptions. With mind management convert pain into pleasure. Mind goes along with the spirit at the time of death, and with its same state, it re-enters a new body in rebirth. One should be always thankful to the harder times of the life, as it makes a being strong and stronger. Never complain about the life, as complaining about the life is complaining about the nature, the existence, the vast creation and the God. Happiness is the by-product of thinking. It is being only, who creates his or her own happiness in his or her life. Stop all worries immediately. Worry does not help. Worries and negativity simply consume up one's mind. These suck him or her completely. Create inner happiness. One's life is what happens inside him or her. Improve your inner, and life will simply improve. Make happiness a habit. Practise positive thinking. Thinking creates feeling. These have empowering effects on the beings. Overthinking is the cause of many worries in the life. Life is neither about positive thinking or negative thinking, and neither it is about overthinking or underthinking, but, it is all about the right thinking. Right thinking is positive thinking. Try to make right conscious decisions in the life. Dreams, goals and aspirations should not become a trap, and must be of right meaning and worth for the life. Dreams, goals, aspirations and decisions to be just right for a being, must be free from all his or her associated influences. Right thoughts lead to right actions and then into the right results. Life is a spin-off of many things and related factors. Mental diarrhoea must be immediately stopped. Still the mind, and then, thoughts will also stop. "Worry" is a painful thought. "Happy" is a pleasure thought. Identify, who you are, from the rest within you. Identification of self, and separation from what is not self, stops the mind from wandering, the worries end then, and the happiness begins.

CHAPTER FIFTY-TWO

Sleep

Positive thoughts bring sound sleep. Sleep binds health and body together. Sleep is a natural healer. Sleep promotes one's physical, mental and emotional health. Sleep brings peace of mind. Peace is the best bed to sleep on. Sleep solves the problems of life. Sleep is a process of slipping into death-state, and going into the lap of the God. Getting awake from sleep is rebirth. Love self; therefore, give a good sound sleep to self. Sleep is the secret of one's internal and external beauty and charm. In sleep, subconscious and unconscious minds are very active, as conscious mind is relaxing. All past life memories and experiences are stored there in the subconscious and the unconscious minds. Sleep is unconscious meditation. Meditation is conscious sleep. The subconscious mind is very powerful, and it has in it, solution of each and every problem of life. One can very easily see his or her past life in dreams in the sleep state. In alert state or wakeful state, brain wave is Theta Wave. In sleep state, which is a relaxed state, brain wave is Alpha Wave. Sleep state is a hypnotic state, therefore, it is suggestible. Thus, it is possible to see the past lives in the sleep state. In sleep state, subconscious mind is active. If once, the subconscious mind receives an instruction, it immediately starts working on it, and then manifests that thing in the life. In meditation, brain relaxes, but remains fully alert. In the state of meditation, brain wave is Delta Wave. Heart Rate and Metabolism both, slow down during Meditation. In the state of deep meditation, autosuggestion given to the mind is well accepted, and its imagery is then created. Autosuggestion is hypnotic or subconscious adoption of an idea, which one has originated oneself. In the body, there is a Pineal Gland, which is located deep inside the brain in an area, known as Epithalamus. Epithalamus is the area, where the two halves of the brain join with one another. Pineal Gland is the Third Eye. Do "Third Eye Meditation". Third Eye is very powerful. Third Eye Chakra is the sixth Chakra of the body, below the Crown Chakra, and above the Throat Chakra. Third Eye Chakra is located in the centre of head, parallel to the middle of eyebrows. Third Eye Chakra is linked with perception, awareness, and spiritual communication. When Third Eye is opened or activated, it provides wisdom and insight, and deepens the spiritual connection. Stop calcification of the Pineal Gland or the Third Eye, through its activation, by doing Third Eye Meditation. The "Third Eye Activation" results in increased levels of awareness, which transcends time and space. If Third Eye is activated, one can easily see his or her past and future, and also, of the others. The Pineal Gland secretes a hormone, called as Melatonin. Melatonin is vertebrate hormone "$C_{13}H_{16}N_2O_2$". Melatonin is derived from Serotonin. Pineal Gland secretes Melatonin in response to darkness. Melatonin regulates Circadian Rhythm. Circadian Rhythm is the natural cycle of physical, mental, and behavioural aspects within the body in a twenty four hours cycle. Sleep is a blessing of life. Live a blessed life by having good sound sleep. Before going to bed, calm the mind by some relaxation techniques or by meditation, and soothe the body by taking a shower of lukewarm water. Clean the bed and make it tidy. Think positive, listen to mind-calming music, and then slowly slip into the sleep state. Good quality of sleep is the secret of a good quality of life.

CHAPTER FIFTY-THREE

Real Beauty

Beauty is the quality, which gives pleasure to the senses. Beauty is an expression of pleasure, satisfaction, contentment, wellness, and the happiness. One should always remain in the state of being beautiful. Real beauty is the light of the heart. In this vast creation, everything has its own charm and beauty. Nature is beautiful. The God is the ultimate beauty. One's real inner beauty is always too captivating. Beauty is the illumination of the soul. Keep smiling, as it makes one beautiful. A beautiful being has a very strong aura. Beauty brings confidence. Positive thinking is the dose of beauty. Essentially, the power of beauty is the power of positive thinking. Beauty is reflected in one's thoughts, actions, and the behaviour. Beauty brings joy and bliss in the life. In nature, everything is too beautiful. Look at the hills and the mountains, rivers and the valleys, sun and the moon, birds, rainbow, waterfall, birds, butterflies, flowers etc., and try becoming them, in order to become beautiful. Be a giver in the life with no expectations. Beauty is always internal, and never external. External beauty is a deception. Beauty is the characteristic of the soul. This creation is too beautiful. Creation holds the beauty of its creator, the God. Beauty lies in the eyes of the beholder. Only the eyes filled with love, can find beauty within the things. Real beauty of a being, make him or her fearless and strong. Real beauty is linked to one's character. Beauty is a simple reality of the life. Being honest and genuine, make a being beautiful. Beauty is an experience and a created belief. In the nature, try finding the beauty of light, sound, colours, shape, size and smell. If these are found, and learnt, these will eventually make the being beautiful. Life is too beautiful. Life is a gift by the nature. Love the life. Admire, care and protect the life. Beauty is the signature of the God. If real beauty is found, God is found. Beings having sweet relationships are beautiful in reality. Beauty is eternal in nature. Beauty is not temporary, but permanent. Beauty is never relative, but always absolute. Be with the nature, act according to the nature, and in turn, nature will make you beautiful. Real beauty is natural, and not artificial. Search of divinity within, and its attainment, makes the being beautiful. Beauty is power in itself. Beauty shines even in the presence of flaws and the odds. Be patient, in order to become and stay beautiful. Learn to accept and appreciate the harsh realities of the life in order to become beautiful. Be simple in everything. "Simplicity" simply leads to the higher levels of beauty.

CHAPTER FIFTY-FOUR

The God

Thoughts, feelings and the imaginations have been bestowed upon the beings, by the God, in order to lead a great and a fulfilling life. God is the energy of the universe(s). God created this infinite creation. Every entity here is an element of the universal energy, i.e. the God. The God is the creator, sustainer, saviour, and also, the destroyer. The God can be very easily found in the silence and the meditation. The God can be easily found in the nature. Trust the timings of the God. God fights the battles of beings, and continuously makes the way(s) in order to come out it. Pray to the God. God listens to every earnest prayer. Keep the mind still and calm. God is peace, and the peace is the God. For every being, for his or her every journey of life, the God makes a beautiful plan of his or her journey of life. Every day is beautiful. Every moment is beautiful. Leave all the choices with the God, and the God will give the best. Spend some time every day to sharpen the mind. Heal all the emotional pains. Every big event in the life is the will of the God. Respect it, and accept it. It is definitely for a better future. Certainly, there is a beautiful bigger picture. Trust, hope, belief and patience are the mantras for a happy, meaningful, gratifying and fulfilling life. All beings are the figments of imagination of the God. Be a god-realised being in the life. Realisation of the God, gives enlightenment, and tells the true nature of the life. God is everything. Everything is God. This creation is an outcome of play of energies. Energies of universe are controlled by a supreme energy. These energies are gods, and the supreme energy coordinating and controlling all these energies, is the God. Fire, light, wind, water, sound etc., are the energies and the powers of the universe. These energies and powers are gods. Thought about is the God is always too invigorating. It is the best positive thought with largest or the highest power among the powers of all other positive thoughts. God's knowledge is eternal. The knowledge of the God-realisation is non-sectarian. The God is outside, and also, inside. Give all the pains and pleasure to the God, and just witness the life, the way it goes. Make best possible sincere efforts without serious expectations. Results are given by the God. Efforts are to be made by the beings. God is the vibration of the universe. In essence, there is only one mind, and any apparent multiplicity is non-real, simply an illusion. The supreme, i.e. the God has no dual, and it is only one. We all are the children of the God, then why to worry. Just lead a good life, and accept whatever comes in its way, with humility, grace and full decency.

CHAPTER FIFTY-FIVE

Death And Beyond

After physical death, there is a definite life between lives (LBL), an afterlife, and a sure rebirth. In this creation, everything is being recycled, and every process is cyclic in nature. Birth-Death-Rebirth is also a cyclic process of creation, then destruction, and then re-creation. Same thing is being returned again and again with certain transformations in the show of life in this creation. After physical death, spirit goes to the Spirit World, which is a yet another different dimension with relatively higher level of vibrations. Time moves very slowly there in the Spirit World. In the Physical World (earth), the level of vibrations as compared to the Spirit World is low, but the times moves faster. Life is a play of matter and energy. Beings and other entities are produced as the consequence of this play (interaction of energy and matter (material)). We are not life, but we only contribute in the play of the life, as a character for a very short time, with certain aims, objectives, goals and the very purpose. Death is the part of the life. Death is a goodbye, which does not say that we will not meet now, but simply says that we meet sometime later again. Death is the state of peace of soul or the spirit. Death is a long and complete sleep. Death should be peaceful. Do not count the life for its worth by its length, but count it by its depth. Do not lead a vegetative life. Death occurs due to the matter. Matter decays. Energy never decays. In essence, beings are energies, i.e. soul or the spirit, and definitely not the matter (physical body). Physical body is the temporary house or the cover of the soul or the spirit. Soul or the spirit comes into a body, thereby, initiating a birth of a being, in order to gain the experiences, settle its past karma, and evolve and advance. Karma is the basis of the whole creation. Karma is, change(s) which get(s) created in one's energyscape due to his or her thoughts and actions in lifetime(s). The energy has to come to its equilibrium, which is the nature of energy i.e. the Law of Equilibrium, therefore, birth, death, and then again birth (rebirth) occur. Some old negative karma is settled in every lifetime, but unfortunately, due to the lack of conscious thoughts and actions, some new negative karma is also earned in the same lifetime, which becomes of the basis for next birth i.e. rebirth. When this karma is fully settled, i.e. there are no upheavals and other disturbances in one's energyscape, then, there is no further birth (rebirths). It is the state of spirit's complete dissolution, i.e. Moksha. It is the state of integration of being's soul with the supreme soul, i.e. the God. Death must be peaceful and graceful. Death is an act of exit, the exit of soul or spirit from the body, and this act of exit should be dignified. Learn the art of death. Death is an honour of life. Death is also an act of the God, similar to the birth. Every death of a normal being happens for a next birth, i.e. rebirth. Time and space play a very important role in the birth, the journey of life, the death and the rebirth. Death is not an end. Death is the awakening. After death, the soul or the spirit moves to the Spirit World. Spirit World has a definite model of governance, with its definite laws. During the stay in the

Spirit World, the spirit is healed, and again made ready for next descend on the physical plane (earth), and thus, creating a new birth of a new old being in the Physical World. It is the power of positive thinking, which helps a being to face and accept the death with aplomb. Positive thinking helps a being to understand the life in a much better way, and thus, leading it in a more meaningful and contented way.

CHAPTER FIFTY-SIX

Positive Thinking, Moksha And Life

Positive thinking is the way of life; rather it is the life itself. Positive thinking is invigorating. Negative thinking is enervating, and too detrimental. Positive thinking gives contentment, happiness and meaning to the life. Positive thinking adds sweetness in the relationships. Positive thinking increases efficiency, improves performance, and brings the desired results in the life. Positive thinking gives a meaning to everything, which is happening in the life, and also to the life. Positive thinking is all-powerful. Life itself has no meaning, but it carries opportunities galore in it, in order to give it (Life), a meaning. Love, care and respect the body, when it is asking for a break. Love, care and respect the mind, when it is seeking rest. Honour the self, and provide it moments and time, in the journey of life. Anything beyond the necessity is simply a poison. Poisons of life are ambition, power, vanity, laziness, fear, food, ego and anger. Be simple, honest, clear and straight. Telling, and listening the truth are quite difficult. Sycophancy is very easy. False and fake is always easy. Moksha releases a being from the cycle of birth-death-rebirth. Moksha is impelled by the Law of Karma. Karma is being's thoughts and actions. Live in the present moment, and then, the life becomes simply better. Life is eternal. It will go on forever. Good or bad life depends on one's quality of thoughts and actions. We are the makers of our own lives. We write our own destinies. Mentally remove everything, and live free. It is a divine life. Moksha is simply a state of conflict-free mind. Lead a good life, and die peacefully, in order to positively impact the next journey of life. Moksha is the realisation of the truth. One can easily control a larger proportion of his or her life. Life is beautiful. Life is mystery. Life is a game. Life is the gift of the God. Birth and death are beyond control for a normal being. Therefore, for normal beings, the only option left is, to lead a good life, based on positive thinking. We all had been here innumerable life times before, and will keep on coming in future also, in different roles, at different times and spaces, as per the will of the God. God is the energy of the universe. Moksha gives liberation from the shackles of birth-death-rebirth. We all are caught and trapped here. Trap is created by the mind. Mind confines the beings. Also, the mind liberates the beings. Positive thinking uses the mind in the right direction. Always be happy, satisfied and peaceful. In life, no gain is a gain, and no loss is actually a loss. This world, and everything here, is ephemeral and illusory. Nothing is for real here. Change is the only constant here. Uncertainty is the only certainty here. Birth, and then, the journey of life, is a trial, a punishment. Therefore, at the death, be conscious, and die consciously. Die in peace, in order to rest in peace. A being, which has not died in peace, can never rest in peace. A wish works, only when it is worked upon, otherwise, these are simply the words of sycophancy and pseudo-relaxation. Love the nature. Live the nature's way. Do not try to be something else, which you are not. Be an unassuming personality. You are best in your present form, as created. No other being can evaluate you. Evaluate the self by yourself. Every day in the life must be better than the day before, and there should be a perceptible incremental improvement. Do not try to understand the life, till you are not sincere about this seeking. A normal being cannot comprehend the life. Play lots of sports. Do lots physical exercises. Walk and run. Eat pure and quality food. Drink lots of water. Do meditation and yoga. Pray to the God with the highest possible purity of the heart. Prayers are listened, when done this way. God is very easily experienced. Connect with the spirits, and also, with the Spirit Guide for help, support and guidance in the journey of life. Activate the third eye. Listen to the gut. Express your gratitude to the nature, this vast existence and creation, and the God. God is the parent of parents. Love and respect your parents. Always be polite and respectful with all. Exchange pleasantries effusively. Keep an open mind. Karma entangles, but the Dharma (the religion) liberates, therefore, follow the right religion in the life. The path of Dharma is the only path to lead a good, moralistic and the pious life. Dharma is the path based on positive thinking. Create a balance in the life. Be like a tree. Always stay grounded, no matter what you get and / or what you become. Always stay connected with your roots in order to stay. Turn over a new leaf, and make a new beginning with the time. Bend before you break. Be humble, as a folded hand has the force to affect the millions. Enjoy your unique natural beauty, you are most beautiful, as you have been created by the God. And, keep growing. Learn all this from a tree. Live for self, and also, for others. Let things happen in the life. Do not try controlling their happening, but simply respond to them wisely. Face them with courage. Time also needs time to create effects. Have faith and belief and patience, and then, universe works for you, and brings the things desired and best deserved.

www.ingramcontent.com/pod-product-compliance
Ingram Content Group UK Ltd.
Pitfield, Milton Keynes, MK11 3LW, UK
UKHW021649190726
13853UKWH00001B/152

9 798885 210263